CONTINUOUS FLAME
A TRIBUTE TO PHILIP WHALEN

Continuous Flame
A Tribute to Philip Whalen

EDITED BY
MICHAEL ROTHENBERG & SUZI WINSON

CONTINUOUS FLAME: A TRIBUTE TO PHILIP WHALEN
FISH DRUM ™ Volume 18/19
© 2004 by Suzi Winson
all rights revert to authors upon publication

Publisher: Fish Drum, Inc.
Editors: Suzi Winson, Michael Rothenberg
Art Direction / Design: Brad Miskell
Web Macher: Ulrich Leschak
Editorial Assistants: Julie Winson, Mani Tyler, Bill Garrity, Arlie Hart
Intern: Font LeRoi
Founding Editor: Robert Winson (1959-1995)

FISH DRUM
P.O. Box 966
Murray Hill Station
New York, NY 10156

ISBN 1-929495-07-2
ISSN 1051-1695

Library of Congress number: 2004111894

A fish drum, or mokugyo, is a slit drum carved into a stylized fish used to accompany chanting in a Zen service.

Printed by Delta Printing, CA.

cover photo: Philip Whalen at San Francisco Zen Center, Page Street, 1973 photographer unknown "... some friend of Lew Ellingham...", said PW

Inside front and back cover art by Philip Whalen

Magazine Distribution by DeBoer of Nutley, NJ.

Subscriptions to Fish Drum Magazine are $24 dollars for 4 regular issues. Send to address above. Subscribers to Fish Drum Magazine get this special book in lieu of 2 regular issues. Stores may sell this as a book or a magazine, whichever suits. When ordering directly from Fish Drum, Inc., please enclose $20 for the issue and a few extra $ for S & H. Ask for special prices for library or bulk orders.

Please refer to page 152 for editor notes and acknowledgements.

FISH DRUM MAGAZINE is an imprint of FISH DRUM, INC.

Check us out at www.fishdrum.com

abbie winson
RED CABBAGE SALAD FOR PHILIP

TABLE OF CONTENTS

PHOTOGRAPHS
(by page number)

suzi winson
PUBLISHER'S NOTE

I met Philip Whalen in the mid-1980's in New Mexico. My brother Robert Winson and Philip were part of a tiny band of Zen practitioners that followed Richard Baker-roshi to Santa Fe from San Francisco Zen Center. They set up shop at the Cerro Gordo Temple and continued what Robert referred to as "Zen Biz": sitting meditation, lectures, cooking, much silence and even more talking. Robert was entirely devoted to Philip. I got to share in his burning literary and historical curiosity about all things "Philip". Letters and phone calls from Robert were peppered with PW news and quips. "...Philip's response to a conversation about Helen of Troy was to utter, 'yes, and Plaster of Paris'..." or, "...Philip said, poetry isn't about delicate discriminations, it's about INTERESTING discriminations, damn it..." or "Philip says we should save all sentient beings...for later!..."

I started plowing through his considerable body of work. I made a desert exodus a half a dozen times in the late 80's elaborating on my own fascination with Philip. I was struck by the texture of his original mind and as well developed a little crush on the bald, cheery/cranky, affectionate, hilarious, egg-shaped priest. I found him daring and necessary.

Philip Whalen was a "Beat" poet, Zen Buddhist monk, abbot, teacher, original thinker and key figure in the literary canon of the second half of the twentieth century. To put him into historical context, PW hailed from Portland Oregon. He was drafted in 1943 into the U.S. Army and later went to Reed College on the G.I. Bill where he met up with poets Gary Snyder and Lew Welch. By the fifties, the three wound up in the Bay Area encountering Allen Ginsberg, Jack Kerouac, Michael McClure, Jack Spicer, Robert Duncan, and Joanne Kyger to name a few, and the explosive American poetry revolution began. He is credited by some as one of the progenitors of both the Language School poetry movement and of Zen poetry in America. He published his first major book of poems in 1960, *Like I Say*. He was perhaps the wisest and wittiest of his cronies and surely the most elegant with vast resources of literary and historical knowledge at his fingertips. Philip wrote dozens of books of poetry and two novels in over 40 years, including *On Bear's Head, The Diamond Noodle, You Didn't Even Try, Canoeing up Cabarga Creek, Overtime: Selected Poems* and *Goofbook*.

Philip and my brother Robert had a long, atypical Talmudic / fast-food relationship of talking Zen and chomping down French fries. Deep practice and recreational eating. Philip was his favorite project. As Philip returned to San Francisco to be the abbot of Hartford Street Zen Center and Robert stayed with his teacher, joy alternated with fear as Philip had a string of medical disasters which kept Robert hopping on airplanes, terrified that Philip was going to die. Ironically, my brother predeceased Philip by 7 years. I took up some of Robert's anxiety and love quotient for PW and sought out talk and food of my own. I dropped in on Philip at Hartford Street (I live in New York) and said "I hear you're a hot lunch date". He smiled to himself and squired me to a Thai place around the corner, hopping slightly from foot to foot rhythmically like an improbably shaped retired ballroom dancer. He asked me to sing him the menu. I was a bit nervous so I obliged quickly and crooned out the appetizers before I realized he was putting me on. "I had heard you could sing," he said. Later he escorted me to a careful miniature garden behind the zendo, explaining each planted item which was amazing since at that point in the late 90's, Philip was virtually blind.

I made a few more trips, corresponded, sent him money for his "peanut brittle and dentist fund". In some elaborate PW health emergency, I hooked up with Michael Rothenberg with whom I'd been leading a parallel life. We were both writer/publishers. We were both trying to look out for Philip. Michael and I became friends in about 5 seconds. We brought Philip salami and a cashmere hat. We arranged for "Phil sitters", priest friends to hang out with him and rub his feet. We crunched itsy-bitsy poetry dollars. Michael co-founded and I joined in to what would be the beginning of Poets In Need which gives Whalen Grants to needy poets.

We kicked around the idea of a tribute, an homage. Michael solicited, I cut and pasted. We sweat a lot. Brad Miskell, my best art-pal shaped the works on the pages and made them sing. Life and death interfered, as it does when you're trying to work, including Philip's own death, as we continued to threaten to do this project. Many thank yous to Philip's friends: a collection of writers, visual artists, publishers, doctors, students, family, et al., many of whom contributed to these pages. Thank you to Bill Berkson and Joe Le Sueur who's *Homage to Frank O'Hara* set a high standard for tributes on paper. Kudos to Michael Rothenberg. Love to Philip.

From PW in 1977, "...Today, I have my head to shave/ There are lights and shadows in it/ All too soon empty open ashes/ Join mirthfully to earth."

PHILIP WHALEN
20.X.23 - 26.Vl.02

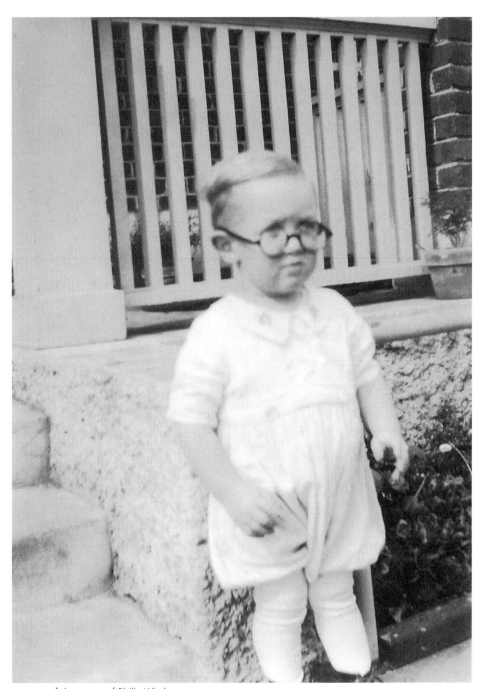

courtesy of the estate of Philip Whalen

robert creeley
HICCUPS
FOR PHIL

It all goes round,
nothing lost, nothing found —
a common ground.

Outside is in,
that's where it all begins
and where it seems to end.

An ample circle
with center full
of all that's in this world —

or that one —
or still another someone
else had thought was fun.

An echo, a genial emptiness,
a finally common place, a bliss
of this and this and this.

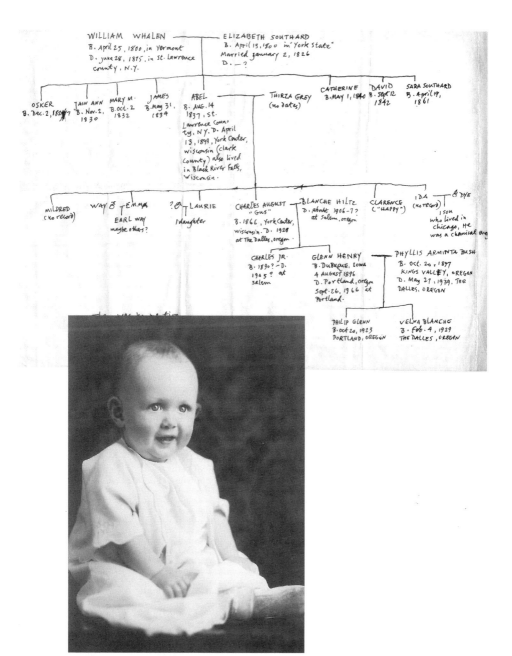

WILLIAM WHALEN
B. April 25, 1800, in Vermont
D. June 28, 1875, in St. Lawrence county, N.Y.

ELIZABETH SOUTHARD
B. April 13, 1800 in "York State"
Married January 2, 1826
D. — ?

OSKER
B. Dec. 2, 1827

JAIN ANN
B. Nov. 2, 1830

MARY M.
B. Oct. 2, 1832

JAMES
B. May 31, 1834

ABEL
B. Aug. 14, 1837, St. Lawrence County, N.Y. D. April 13, 1899, York Center, Wisconsin (Clark County) also lived in Black River Falls, Wisconsin.

THIRZA GREY
(no dates)

CATHERINE
B. May 1, 1840

DAVID
B. Sept 12, 1842

SARA SOUTHARD
B. April 19, 1861

MILDRED
(no record)

WAY & EMMA
EARL WAY
maybe others?

? & LAURIE
1 daughter

CHARLES AUGUST
"Gus"
B. 1866, York Center, Wisconsin. D. 1928 at The Dalles, Oregon

BLANCHE HILTZ
D. about 1906-7? at Salem, Oregon

CLARENCE
("HAPPY")

IDA
(no record)
1 son who lived in Chicago. He was a chemical eng

& DYE

CHARLES JR.
B. 1890? - D. 1905? at Salem

GLENN HENRY
B. Dubuque, Iowa
4 August 1896
D. Portland, Oregon
Sept. 26, 1966 at Portland.

PHYLLIS ARMINTA BUSH
B. Oct. 20, 1897
KINGS VALLEY, OREGON
D. May 27, 1939. THE DALLES, OREGON

PHILIP GLENN
B. Oct 20, 1923
PORTLAND, OREGON

VELVA BLANCHE
B. Feb. 4, 1929
THE DALLES, OREGON

courtesy of the estate of Philip Whalen

courtesy of the estate of Philip Whalen

Dream PW (so recent past is 'to try to' 'wreck one's mind' (by) placing states together which can't exist at the same time) is to be transported out (of danger) by the resistance ('behind the lines'), guerilla fighters — I've dropped him off (I'm remaining behind) and he's waiting on a bench, the pick-up truck (AG driving, whom I don't know very well but who doesn't think) there (by high embanked dirt curbs). Packed with a small bundle. I look to see if he gets in the pick-up, which he will.

Later waking, the important thing is I have no sense of *my* leaving (though he is). Waking see the dirt streets Rangoon, where I was as
a kid for short time — so that it won't exist again (or continue).

Waking, the dream is two events at the same time — being in Rangoon almost a child, with only a sibling, in utter freedom
which hadn't been in my mind in the dream.

To be the outside — in real-time I'm exhausted in that
everything outside is to be translated *thought as convention* — I was trying to translate 'there not being an instant between two instances' as a thought so as to be that action only. But trying is stringing me out.
so the dream is — to translate at the same time. — and is the two at once

the dream is, almost child (no longer existing) in utter freedom *then*

is unknown in the dream, yet *is it,* and
is the same time as *to translate as it* — only which
is a thought but *not* constructing that social existing
that's here (here, the outside is, what thought *is*)

the dream's utter freedom

Walking in Mongolia in fact on vast gold ground as if it illumines the dark
indigo sky, its day-cobalt. So it wasn't night or day time that separates,
or the huge gold plain on which I was walking — it didn't separate
from dark dark blue that's illuminated from it (the plain). There were
no trees. Invisible birds sang.

courtesy of the estate of Philip Whalen

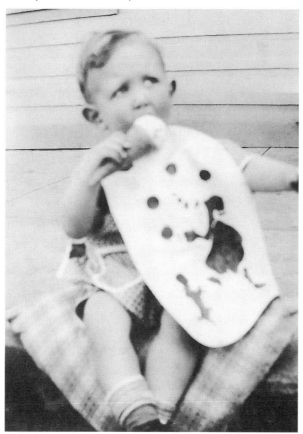

courtesy of the estate of Philip Whalen

7

anselm hollo
2 from GUESTS OF SPACE
TO PHILIP WHALEN

"How is it far if you can think of it?"
It's still far. Sometimes too far. Too far
To even think of —
So let's do the outer space shuffle
On this space shuttle

& think of some more something
In small but sweet helpings ...

        "O dear love I'm so glad
        You did not have to escape
        To that Plywood Motel!"

    Signed, The American Pebble

No, you can't sign that — who *are* you, anyway?

"I'm The American Pebble, author of
The 100 Best-Loved Poems of the American Pebble"

* * * * * * *

here have I summed my sighs, playing cards with the dead
in a broke-down shack on the old memory banks
e'en though my thoughts like hounds
pursue me through swift speedy time
feathered with flying hours
but could have sat there for many more hours
listened to poet friends reading
words by an absent friend whose work we love
in the name of Annah the Allmaiziful,
the Everliving, the bringer of plurabilities
concretized, concertized, temporarily minute
progressions of actions, swirling mists of the past
"you have a lot of stuff here, you know?"
"yes   now run on home"

Seaside, 3 years, 8 months, July 1927
courtesy of the estate of Philip Whalen

The Dalles
courtesy of the estate of Philip Whalen

donald guravich
BUCK ROGERS

duncan mcnaughton
TO PHILIP WHALEN

1. Ishmael's father, you see
          came into the valley of Mecca
    that's what they say,
                to see his son's mother again
          though they don't say that, do they?
          missing as he did her
                      little beauty of ears
          momensity of breasts, of nipples
                their delivery of green light

    but from which direction he came
                they do not tell, as
          its hour wants simple location
        wandering as sin does
                out through the tear in the membrane

2. labyrinthos poikilos
                            changeable   in motion
                the floor of it   its floruit

    had I neglected I had to evert the boundary
                      of its physical space
                unaware of its distribution of sights
                senza areality

    a mistake I had made, a misuse in
                historical geography that Sauer had warned of
          literalization, an ethical gaffe

3. 'I shall,' said Ishmael's father, 'walk
          between her, all along the floor

        of her, of her continent
          to the tower of her hour

     word cut loose / blown through the rip
      in the membrane I shall call
        Tartaros, that
    intermediation of paternity
       inside-out
    pilot of the migration of time

     how many men are the man I am
       blown through the rent
         in the tent
        toward the light beyond, nipple green?'

4.   along the floor the minotaur walks
        cold old floor of polity and rhyme

'I am here,' he tells me, 'simply because
    I had never permission to leave
I have,' going on, 'my particular appearance
    because my mother had been by Aphrodite
      overwhelmed by lust for a snowy white bull

   Pasiphae's child, older now than she
     crippled as you see
   almost blind, my eyes tough to make out
      who visits me now
    what brings you onto this ward?'

To which I reply, 'I have blundered
    back on to it equating as I had
      Crete with far enough west'

   'Reasonable... they too came back to it
     from when they had already been
      the loop of their alphabet's voyage
     brought them here
        from older Erythrean ports...

Say, can you draw a woman for me?'

'I can only draw a stone.'

'That will do. She went out
where she'll come in
the great gate will open
Bab al-'Amud...

can you guess my name?'

'Labrunie?'

'O save me the effort of smiling, it hurts
I suppose that pipsqueak on your shoulder
is Harry Heine!'

Philip with his father, Glenn Henry Whalen
courtesy of the estate of Philip Whalen

michael rothenberg
INTERVIEW

Michael Rothenberg interview with Philip's sister Velna Whalen in San Diego, September 5, 2002, excerpted from "The Real & False Journals"

MR: You know what interests me is what it was like growing up where you grew up, growing up with Philip, your family, that period of time.

VW: We grew up in the 20's, 30's and 40's, in The Dalles, Oregon, a small town. It was a real small town then, but it's a large town now. And there were football games, school, grade school and. . .

Did Philip ever play sports?

No, Pat never played sports. He was more into theatre and reading and going to the library, getting stacks of books, bringing them home, and reading them. Also he played the piano a lot and he played the violin.

You told me he played the piano for your father.

Yes, he played the piano. And my mother and father used to sing while he played, 'cause a lot of people liked to hear my dad sing, and my mom sing. He used to play a lot of classical pieces. He was quite good. I learned a lot about music, although, I never did do anything like that. But I learned a lot. I liked it.

You were five years old.

Yes, I wasn't very old then. Gee, I was five years younger. So, I wasn't quite up to that yet, that stage.

He definitely treated you like a sister.

Yeah, I followed him around. I used to bug him to death. (laughs). I used to pester him. He used to get irritated with me a lot. He used to have chess games in the basement and I used to pester him. And he got mad at me. (laughs).

Did he have a lot of friends when he was young?

He had quite a few. I thought. Yeah, he did have quite a few friends that came over. He'd play the piano. Or they'd play chess. Or something like that, you know.

Your mother passed away when you were a kid.

When I was ten years old she passed away. That was in 1939. Pat was 15, then.

And your grandmother.

Then my grandmother came and took care of us for awhile. She got very sick. She died. Then I went to my aunt's to live. My dad took me over to aunt's to live, in Independence. I stayed there until I went into the service in 1950. Pat was out of the service by then. He was going to Reed, I think. I think he started in Reed College, then. Because he graduated in 1951.

Did you know his friends when he was in college?

No, I never met any of his friends in college. I don't remember any of them.

So when did you stop being around each other on a regular basis?

When I lived with my aunt. I never saw him much at all. Just when I went to Portland to my dad's like holidays, maybe I would see him. That was the only time.

Then you corresponded over the years?

Yes.

When was the last time you saw him?

The last time I saw him was here in San Diego, what was the year, 1980, I think, the year he was here at a poetry reading up in University of San Diego.

So what about your mother?

Well, she was sick a lot, too. My mother, yeah, she always seemed to be sick a lot, to me. What I understand she died of Peritonitis. Infection. That's all I ever knew, could understand (lights cigarette). Yeah, my dad made her sick, all the time, you now…

Stress over his drinking?

Yeah, probably, I don't know, but so many people liked her.

That must have gotten you a little bit jittery, waiting for the other shoe to drop.

Yeah. I remember one time Mom traipsed us down to the train station, one day (laughs) and that was because she was leaving. But as far as I can remember we didn't get on the train. We came back home. So he must have come after us. (laughs). So there were times where she did leave.

Did you guys talk about it?

I don't remember ever talking about it. We always used to joke about it mostly. You know kids. Just, "Oh, he's three sheets in the wind again."

Did you talk about it later?

No, I don't ever remember talking about it at all with him. I guess it was a matter of forgetting. Wanting to forget it, you know, the past. Forgetting that past, getting on with it. Getting on with other things.

I saw a picture of Philip, all these pictures of you two hanging on to each other.

Yeah, that's me, I was always hanging on to him. Big pest.

But what was it? He was your brother, so I understand that. You loved your brother. But what was it? Did you feel safe around him?

Well he was always going some place interesting, or doing things interesting. I wanted to get out. I was always a really bad kid.

So where was Philip going?

Well, I guess, he was going to the library. He took me to the movies. We went to the movies a lot. We walked down the hill. The Dalles was really hilly. Went down to the corner store. Get some Cracker Jacks. Then go to the movie. I think it was a nickel then, a dime. Go to the Sunday matinees. I think it was a Sunday afternoon.

What kind of movies?

Anything that was on. Carole Lombard. Clark Gable.

I saw he sent you autographs of Carole Lombard and Marlene Dietrich from the USO?

Yeah, that's where he went one evening. He got to meet "Fats" Waller, yeah he was very excited about that…He had his own puppet show you know? He built his own stage. He was, gee, I don't know how old he was. I wish I knew but he built his own stage, made his own puppets, *papier mâché,* painted them up. Put on a show. Made up a show. Punch and Judy and he put that on. Some people saw it and they liked it and they wanted him to come to the church and put it on there and he did that. (laugh). It was quite a big project for him. He must have been about 13 or 14.

I've seen pictures of him at Reed in a play.

I saw him in one play in high school, "The Night of January Sixteenth," it was called. He was a judge in that one (laughs). He was good. He was very good. He played the part very well. That's the only one I saw him in. Wait a minute, wait a minute, there was *HMS Pinafore,* I don't remember if he was in that or not, but I loved that one.

Philip was famous for his appetite. You do know that his eating was almost as legendary as his writing.

He used to go out to a hotel in Portland, to this hotel and have this soup. What's it called, French, I can't remember the name. *Bouillabaisse!* I think he attempted to cook. But I can't remember. I know he liked to eat yes, but

I don't remember him eating a lot.

In one picture in a bathing suit, you and him, and you were hanging on to him, he looked like he'd gotten quite plump, there.

We had enough to eat. But I don't remember huge amounts that he would eat. I don't remember that.

He used to drive the hospice people crazy because he would order special food all the time. He was staying in a nice hospice for a long time where everyone liked to cook, they didn't realize he would have them stoking the fire constantly. And many of his friends recall their main job in their relationship would be running food errands.

This must have been later because I don't remember.

Interesting.

I think he liked to cook. I love to eat myself.

There was a big thing of noodles that was put on his altar. And a box of peanut brittle. He loved Mrs. See's peanut brittle.

(Laughs). This is all later.

You say that sitting with him, his quietness...

Yes, he was very quiet. He used to read a lot. I used to be outside all the time, riding the bicycle. He was an indoor man. I used to go up and see how he was doing, Sit and listen.

Did he try to raise you. I see from one letter he gave you instructions on what kind of education you should get, how you should approach school.

I wasn't too good at school. I was lousy.

Was he good in school?

He was very good at school. I always went to him with my arithmetic problems.

So you were the trouble-maker.

I was a tomboy. I was always outdoors playing football or baseball. Or riding a bicycle. He was always in. I don't remember him playing sports or anything.

I always had a hard time imagining him at Sourdough Mt.

Yeah, I was surprised at that.

Seemed like a kind of rough life.

Well, we had this cabin up in Mt Hood, you know, did he tell you about that? My uncle and my dad built it. It was just one big room, big stove, and we put up curtains to close off the beds. A whole bunch of us, whole family, would go up there. We spent a lot of time up there in the summers, mostly in the summers. There were a lot of people up there. He liked the outdoors, the mountains. It was beautiful there. I really enjoyed that. I think that was the best time, up there.

Would you think of him as a happy kid?

(laughs) He was always a *man.* (laughs) I think he was more mature than anything else.

Do you think he took that on because of the family situation, the drinking father?

I think so. He was very concerned. He was always concerned with us, with my mom, myself. That's why I guess…I don't think my dad and him got along at all, very well. He didn't want a job, you know. He didn't want to work, my brother. My dad, he was a workaholic. He didn't like this.

How did Philip explain that?

Well, he didn't. He didn't live very long with my dad. You know, he moved out. He lived in Portland when he was going to Reed.

So as soon as he got out of school he split?

Well, he lived with my dad for awhile in Portland. But then something happened, I don't know what.

He wasn't looking for a career?

No, that wasn't for him.

When did he decide he wanted to be a poet?

Well, I would imagine when he was in Reed College, or before that. I don't remember him speaking about being a poet. The time I knew about it was when he was in college. And, then when he was in the Beat Generation. That's the only time I knew.

It must have been pretty surprising to watch him suddenly come into this whole world.

It was. I was very surprised. But he did.

So it wasn't obviously apparent he was looking for it?

No, I don't think so. No.

He was just reading and living and enjoying the arts.

Enjoying the arts, right.

He was always a kind of sensualist. He liked those things, the arts.

Sure.

Did he have a girlfriend when he was growing up?

He might have had. I don't know. He had a lot of girls around. (laughs). Yeah.

So the girls liked him, huh? Why do you think they liked him?

They liked his personality. He was charming, He was a sweet guy, you know. He was funny. He was serious. He was a real serious guy.

He liked having women around. He liked their company. He always seemed to be able to build confidences. Men and women.

michael rothenberg   19

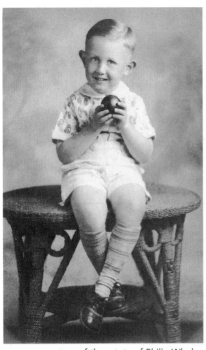

courtesy of the estate of Philip Whalen

Philip holding 3-month-old sister Velna
courtesy of the estate of Philip Whalen

Philip with Velna, 1933 or '34,
in front of 119 W 11th St. in The Dalles.
courtesy of the estate of Philip Whalen

Philip with his mother, Phyllis Armenta Bush Whalen
and Velna. courtesy of the estate of Philip Whalen

Philip with Velna early 1945
courtesy of the estate of Philip Whalen

Yeah, everybody in the family liked him. (lights a cigarette)

People always ask me why he didn't get married. It never seemed that important.

I never asked him, myself. I never thought about it.

Maybe it was his shyness.

That could be. He was shy. Quiet…Well, my mother was quiet too. Like that. She was quiet too. They were pretty close, my mother and brother, very close.

Do you know that poem he wrote that includes the Letter to Mama?

No, I don't. He really loved her. She was a good woman, too. She was a good person. A real good person. She put up with a lot.

So she encouraged you.

She never pushed any, one way or the other, that I can remember.

So was Philip just one of the kids? Or did he stand out?

Well, he wasn't like a football type. He was just another regular kid. Some of the guys kind of teased him, I think.

Because he was bookish?

Yeah. But, he got along alright. You know, didn't get in any fights or anything.

He could match them in wits.

Yeah, that's right.

So a lot of your life contact was strictly through correspondence.

That's right.

He kept in contact with you. He called you a lot?

Well, no, not on the phone. Cause we never had a phone on the farm. But in town we had a phone but he never called there. I don't remember him calling.

Mostly writing?

Yeah, mostly writing. I was so glad to get his letters and hear from him because I was lonely on the farm. And in town where we moved from the farm, I was at a stage. I wasn't very happy anyway. I was living with my aunt and uncle. Nan, I never got along with her. But, that's one of the reasons. I went into the service, is to get out of that misery I was in. I got into another misery in the army.

But maybe there were lots of people there feeling miserable like you.

I enjoyed the service. It was alright. I met a lot of people. Yeah. It was worthwhile.

You went to Service, and Philip was…

In Reed at that time.

And the beat stuff had not started.

I was in New York by then. I was living in Tarrytown. Then we moved down to New York. In Brooklyn.

Your father knew what was going on?

I have no idea.

Did you continue to keep in contact with your father?

I did. I wrote once in a while.

Did he ever comment about Philip's work, or acknowledge him?

He never acknowledged anything that I remember. He died in 1965. I sort of separated myself from family. Which possibly wasn't right…Everybody's gone now.

Do you think Philip ever wanted approval of his father?

I don't think so. I don't think he wanted approval of the family. Or anything like that.

But he was proud to share with you?

I was proud of him. Went down, saw him. In the village. We met him in the Village for coffee. Hard to remember so long ago it was in the 50's.

I notice in the letters he talks about having this book coming out, or getting this check, $15.00 and buying a steak he couldn't digest, ended up in the hospital.

I guess the only thing I had on my mind was a job and being able to support myself. That was all I was concerned about at the time. I was just glad he could go ahead and do what he wanted to do. That was his aim in life, was to write poetry.

At Reed, that was a big transformation, yes, as far as knowing what he wanted to do?

I don't know that period too much. I never heard him say he wanted to be a violinist or pianist. Or anything like that. He didn't want a permanent job. I don't blame him. I'm glad he did what he wanted to do and been able to do it. I'm proud of him that he did.

He never seemed to put that burden on anybody else. He always encouraged you to do what you wanted to do. He was like that with me. An encouragement. He never said, go get a real job. If someone was making a big mess and hysterical he might encourage them to get it together.

Well, if you had some talent you needed to project, that needed development…he always encouraged me to read.

I notice you have a lot of books around. A lot of tapes. Movies. Histories. You have a lot of historical things.

History and archeology and stuff like that. Discovery Channel.

Philip liked history.

He was great. He could remember all of those things. I would have liked to have sat down with him more and have him tell me all these things that he knew.

How did he get all those books? Check them out of the library?

Yeah, he'd go down to the public library.

He used to say he couldn't hold on to money. He had to go buy books.

Yeah that was him. He bought a lot of books. I didn't send him too much money. I guess I couldn't afford it then.

Tell me some of your favorite stories of you and Philip. Some trouble.

Oh gosh. I just can't think of anything

Did he ever get in trouble?

Not that I know of. I was always in trouble.

Okay. Tell me.

One day I was coming home from school and I was coming down this alley and this kid threw a rock at me. And I threw a rock back at him. And I went home. My mother heard about it. She took me back down there and made me apologize to the boy. (laugh). But those little things like that I used to get into trouble. (laughs). Let's see what else did I do, terrible things. I'd follow Pat around and he'd tell me to go home. Oh dear.

That really bugged him.

Yeah, that bugged him. Then I'd go to the movies and I'd stay overtime. I'd come out and my mother and father were frantic. I walked home and they'd come home and just about kill me. I shouldn't have walked home, it was dark, I shouldn't have stayed. I stayed to watch a couple of pictures over and over again.

Did they ever send Philip after you?

No.

What was Philip doing while you were starting trouble?

Probably reading away. Reading and writing. Upstairs in his room.

Did he write as a kid?

I don't know if he did…I was always in trouble. Even with the kid next door I got in trouble. I think I hit him, or popped him. I got in trouble over that. My mother had a fit. Oh, god! My brother and mother were pretty well together on things. They knew I was in trouble.

Did Philip always liked to play with names. Where did that come from? You know how he calls you Snook-ookums, and used words like SPLAT. Did you read many comic books as a kid.

Well, we used to exchange comic books with the neighborhood kids. That's where he got that.

I noticed in his library there was a copy of Krazy Kat. He just loved that.

Yeah, he did like *Krazy Kat*. That was one of them. *Katzenjammer Kids.*

And popular songs?

He played them. He played well. He was real good.

You sang them as a family.

Yeah, we could all sing together. My dad sang a lot. (She sings, "On the road to Mandalay"). And Pat would play. Yeah, he would sing them all the time. That was fun.

He seemed connected a lot to that, to his family, very sentimental about that period of his life. Though he was somewhat disconnected from it...

He was.

But he was nostalgic.

Yeah, family and all, I guess.

I guess as kids we kind of overlook, and gloss over our childhood problems. I didn't think much about my father's drinking until I was in my 20's. It didn't really occur to me that my father was an alcoholic until then.

I didn't think too much about it until later too, but I knew that something was getting worse.

We had a bar in the house. My father had a seat behind the bar. And he was the bartender. He'd come home and that was his position. We'd all line up at the bar and say hello. And we'd laugh and he'd drink. We sang a lot as a family. My mother was a very strong woman. We were very close.

Yeah. Same with Pat and my mother.

You know, he spoke with my mother on the telephone. When my mother was sick and he was sick. I was running between my mother and Philip. I just one day got him on the phone, got my mother on the phone and said here, you both know about each other...

Talk.

Right. Which was really great to connect these two important people in my life. Kept wondering who's going to go first.

How long was your mother sick?

Quite awhile. 4 or five years. She had emphysema. It got progressively worse. About the same time as Philip started to get sick. It was hard to tell how things would go with her. Then she got lung cancer and that was quick.

Was your father living?

No, he died from a heart attack... By the way, I remember someone said at the memorial, "Thank you, Philip, for being a grandmother to everyone."

(laughs). That's cute.

A lot of people trusted him. As I looked into his relationship with Jack Kerouac it became evident that Kerouac trusted Philip. People could confide in him. People could tell him their innermost feelings and know it was going to stay there. Confide in him, the PR on Philip was that he was "The High Priest of The Beat Generation." It has a mythical ring.

Yes, That's interesting.

Did you ever think of him as a priest?

Not in my wildest dreams.

You were surprised when he became a monk.

He wasn't a religious person that I ever knew him to be.

As he explained, Buddhism was a religion.

We went to the Christian Science church. My mother was a Christian Scientist. That was the only church we went to. Sunday school and church.

He mentions that in his poems to your mom.

And then when I went to live with my aunt I became a Presbyterian because my uncle was a Presbyterian.

So how did Philip tell you?

He wrote to me and said he was becoming a Buddhist priest. I thought, that's fine, that's good. Good for him.

I know if I had called my home and told them I was going to become a Buddhist priest that would have been the last time my mother spoke to me.

(laughs). My family probably would have done the same, too. Sort have been shocked.

When you talk about Buddhism in this country there is an arrow that points to that crowd of Philip, and Allen, and Gary Snyder, about Buddhism and it's popularization. His generation is said to have ushered Buddhism in to the whole country, when it wasn't very common. Now there's the new age preoccupation with Buddhism, Tibetan Buddhism..

It's become very popular now.

So in a way he almost became a kind of missionary.

Actually, yes. It's amazing. I just never thought of him as being in a religious sect, or anything like that. I've never seen him as a religious person. I've seen him as a man, as a person. But that's why he went to Japan. He was over there a long time too.

Yeah, he was in the crossroads of this change which became known as The Beats. Did he ever talk to you about what he thought the Beat thing was?

I never heard him speak about it, The Beat Generation, that I remember.

He never seemed to care to talk about it.

Maybe he separated himself from it, sort of. Maybe he didn't think he was part of it.

Well there was the New York crowd.

Yeah, he was mostly part of the West Coast.

Well, what about drugs? You know that period.

No drugs that I know of. I don't know if he did. I'm so glad I never got involved with any of that. Who knows, he might have smoked a few, or something. I tried it once, marijuana, didn't care much for it, thank god. I mean I don't care what anybody else does, but just thank God I didn't get into it.

He kept a little bottle of scotch in his closet.

(Laughs). Um, good. A little nip, a little thing that he wanted. Wine or something.

People tried to get him to modify his diet. But he had a good long life. He was 78.

I guess he lived the life that he wanted to live. He was happy with it. That's the main thing. He was happy with his life.

He had a thing I always point out, maybe you can shed some light on. When people are trying to kind of understand his work, I tend to say, if you read Philip's poetry you will see this theme that runs through it, it goes something like this: "Leave me alone! I want to be alone. Leave me alone. I want to be alone. Why am I so alone?" There was a dramatic thrash between not wanting to be alone, but feeling totally bothered by everybody not leaving him alone. Where do think that comes from?

Me pestering him to death. (laughs).

You've been entering this through the whole story. So how much did you pester him?

I used to follow him around all over the place.

For days and years on end?

(laughs) That's probably why he was the way he was. He didn't want to be bothered.

He couldn't get rid of you?

Oh, he had to of course. I couldn't pester him forever.

Well, he must have been fun to have as a brother.

He really was. He had such a sense of humor. We used to goof around.

I actually find his poetry very funny.

Yeah, it really is. (sigh). It doesn't seem possible that he's gone. These people go so fast. People that we want to stay alive forever. But…

It must be very lonely without him.

I think of him often, everyday. Wonder what's he's doing. (laughs).

Still wondering what he's doing. I kind of wonder that. He had a way of getting in your mind. I guess when you trust someone there's nothing to lose by letting them in there. His silence was important.

It was important to him. You need that, really, that silence. Because the world is so hectic. Never-ending.

His silence would drive some people crazy. There were a lot of people who were very afraid of him.

Oh, really, I would never think that.

When he lost his temper he could be pretty loud. Sometimes it was more directed toward the universe than it was toward any individual. Like if he went to hang up his cane or hat and missed the hook he would let out a stream of curses that didn't stop, that echoed through the temple.

Oh, gosh.

I remember the first time I heard that, I thought, you can't do that in a temple. But then after that I thought, Right on! Fine! . . . His silence would make people uneasy, they didn't know what they should say, or shouldn't say, and got all tangled up in that. Was it like that when he was kid?

Gee, I don't think so.

But he was quiet.

Yes.

Was he affectionate?

Yes.

Was he a hugger?

Well, not exactly.

I don't know what affection was in those days.

(Laughs).

So how was he affectionate?

Not showy. He'd just take me by the hand and go to the movies.

So he didn't always chase you off.

No he didn't.

You were his pet.
That's because I was the baby in the family. Spoiled brat.
I saw the letter, he calls you "baby", kitten", snook-ookums",
"droopy". He had a whole stream of affectionate terms.
Droopy, he still called me that.
Well, is there any thing that you can think of that you'd like to say?
I had an enjoyable life as kids. I enjoyed our life as kids. We did so much.
We had a cabin in Mt. Hood. We went to Cannon Beach in the summer.
That was really fun. Fun time that we had. Movies and rock fights and
comic books and playing tag, kick-the-can at night, a bunch of us would go
out at night, and kick-the-can.

*

"White River and rises from the sea
A glacier on Mt. Hood, a river at Government Camp
Creamy thick with stone flour
Outside Tyghe Valley it's clear
A trout stream that my father fished several times a year
Mother found lumps of agate on gravelly shore
Alder, willow, bracken, tarry pines
My sister and I caught crawdads
Icy water cooling beer and melons
      (O Shirakawa, the Kamo River is a god
      Its waters magically turning red and green)
I thought "We'll all stay here forever," but we went home.
Now here's Kyoto Shirakawa the white river again
Flows out of my skull, white sandy ashes of my parents
Water ouzel, dragonfly, crawfish
Blazing trout and bright carnelian jewels
Never so near, never so far from home.
          1:v:66
          23:vi:66

—from White River Ode

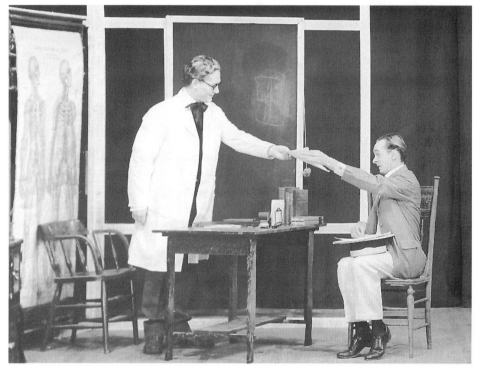

Philip Whalen, actor, 1947
courtesy of the estate of Philip Whalen

gary snyder
HIGHEST AND DRIEST
FOR PHILIP ZENSHIN'S POETIC DRAMA/DHARMA

I first saw Philip from the wings back stage, he was out front in a rehearsal, directing some point with the actors. His confidence and clarity impressed me, a freshman at seventeen, naive and new.

Philip as director and actor for some student production — I heard soon, though, that he wrote poetry and then in conversation later, I was delighted by his erudition and searching wit. We became friends.

Philip had grown up in The Dalles — up the Columbia gorge and at the beginning of the dry side of the ranges, He had been in the Air Force, and had already read much philosophy, literature, and history. Being part of Phil's circle was like being in an additional class — having an extra (intimately friendly) instructor, one with nutty humour and more frankly expressed opinions. He extended us into areas not much handled by the college classes of those days, such as Indian and Chinese philosophy. I had done some reading in the *Upanishads,* had ventured into the *Tao Te Ching* and the Confucian Classics, and was just beginning to read Warren's translations from Pali Buddhist texts. Philip led the way in making conversation possible, and then making poetry out of the territory of those readings. His own poetry circled around and into it a bit, with a dimension that was not quite present in our official modernist mentors Yeats, Pound, Eliot, Williams, and Stevens. (My other close new poet friend in this loose group was Lew Welch.) Philip had an elegant style of speaking with intonations, phrases, and subtle linguistic mannerisms that lightly affected many.

The Chinese-American World War II veteran Charles Leong, brilliant student and expert calligrapher, plus Lloyd Reynolds who taught printing, calligraphy, art, creative writing, William Blake's poetry, and much else — moved in and out of these conversations as well. In some odd way there was already a Pacific Rim post-industrial consciousness in the air then, right in the sleepy backward old Pacific Northwest where the restaurants were either Swedish smorgasbord or things like "The Oyster House." The memories of W.W. I were not totally dried up either; same with the memories of the big old time logging camps and the extravagant earlier salmon runs.

I wasn't writing much poetry yet — but Lew and Phil were, and we all admired it. I didn't begin to write poems that I could relate to until I was in my mid-20s. By that time I'd been briefly in Indiana for graduate school and then back to the Bay Area to live and work on the docks of San Francisco. Philip and I shared an apartment on Montgomery Street, and began to move in cosmopolitan circles of writers and artists of the whole Bay Area: Robert Duncan, Jean Varda, Jack Spicer, Michael McClure and many more. We got to know Alan Watts, met Claude Dalenberg and the McCorkle brothers; and attended the Berkeley Buddhist Church's Friday night study group meetings (Jodo Shin was our first contact with a living Buddhist practice.)

Philip and I would go our separate ways to job opportunities here or there, up and down the whole West Coast, but we would always end up back in San Francisco at some convenient meeting place like Cafe Trieste, or a little later, Kenneth Rexroth's Friday evening salon. Chinese poetics, the flow of Indian Sanskrit poetry, Pound's line, Blake quoted by heart, Gertrude Stein avidly read aloud, Lew Welch singing Shakespeare songs to his own melodies, all led the way toward whatever it was we did next. Like taking up the study and practice of Mah Jong and the *I Ching,* or cross-town walks to the beach and the Legion of Honour. Philip was always writing, always reading, and whenever possible playing music. At one time he went to considerable trouble to get an old pump organ into our apartment, to play Bach on.

Allen Ginsberg and Jack Kerouac came to town, and catalyzed the energy already fully present into a more public poetics and politics. I left for my long residence in Japan. For some years I sent Philip the news of the Capital, until he came there. Once in Kyoto, Philip seemed instantly intimate with the sites of literature and history, commenting that *"here* was where Lady Murasaki had that little altercation with the other lady over which carriage should go first" or some Buddhist temple that had been built on an old palace foundation. Then he began to be drawn more and more to the message of the big Buddhist temples, and the lessons of impermanence their vast graveyards out back provide: thousands of little stupas for the priests of the past. Thus moving from the seductive cultural fascinations of old Japan to a deeply realized *samsaric* awareness. Note well his poetry and prose from the Old Capital. Once back on the West Coast it was not long before he made the step into full Zen practice.

Once a priest, it was clear that this was Philip's true vocation. He had the dignity, the learning, the spiritual penetration, and the playfulness of an archetypal Man of the Cloth, of any tradition, and yet was not in the least tempted by hierarchy or power. Philip never left his poetry, his wit, or his critical intelligence behind; his way of poetry is a main part of his teaching. His quirks became his pointers, and his frailties his teaching method. Philip was always the purest, the highest, the most dry, and oddly cosmic, of the Dharma-poets we've known — we are all greatly karmically lucky to have known him.

Claws / Cause

for Zenshin

"Graph" is graceful claw-curve,
grammar a   weaving carving

paw track, lizard-slither, tumble of
a single boulder down. Glacier scrapes across Montana,
wave-lines on the beach.

Saying, "we were here"
scat sign of time and place

language is   shit, claw, or tongue

"tongue" with all its flickers
might be a word for

hot love, and   fate
A single kiss   a tiny cause [claws]

— such grand effects [text].

30. VIII. 02

Gary Snyder, Philip Whalen and Lew Welch, June 1964
photo by James Hatch "Steamboat"

Gary Snyder and Philip in train en route to Nara Hills, March 12, 1966
photo by Ken Walden

Philip, Joanne Kyger, Jay Blaise, Dave Haselwood & Albert Saijo
(back to camera) at Hyphen House, SF, January 1960
by permission of Joanne Kyger

joanne kyger
"I WANT TO ANSWER ALL YOUR CROOKED QUESTIONS ABSOLUTELY STRAIGHT"
from letters from Philip

20 July 1962

"Poetry is what we do...you liked Wittgenstein's idea of 'doing philosophy'...poetry is the same."

5th October 1962

"Yes it does take nerve, to let people see what you have written, have them hear what you are saying, all of us are ignorant & tied down to the wheels of anguish and repetition...I write & people read it & they can say, why that old phoobie is as silly & dopie as we are...but those who say so enjoy reading it & had not the energy or discipline or nerve to write it down for themselves & so they have no choice except to read me or Pascal or Melville, none of us good but exceedingly charming & foolish men. & that is literature. Or something. I get a kick out of writing. On days it isn't fun I do something else."

9 April 1963

"Please just sit down and WRITE some every day, and continue to have your own peculiar kind of vision, it is quite comprehensive enough. It will change as you read more and see more and live longer, all of us do change in time, for better or for worse, we do practice at being hopefully better, but even that is possibly a waste of time, we do try to pay more attention and compassion, that's all I know for sure. I think 'form' is for crystals or for the thing after it has been seen. Ok, form it or arrange it to suit your vision, if that's how you want to spend your afternoons; the things ALREADY have a shape, Ginsberg is absolutely right, 'MIND IS SHAPELY, ART IS SHAPELY'."

31 January '63

"I am not at the moment in a rage but could possibly fly into one at any moment if it would amuse you."

reed bye
EARHOUSE, P.W.

Like a shipment of beams
        or slabs swinging into a warehouse
                from a crane, on a chain

at just the moment
        the man in the cab
                cuts the current

        the heavy weight lands like a starling

on skids. "You got it, Phil"
        you got it down

in words.   Like a long spring rain

flushing worms from the soil

or a banked stream
tossing up refuse—
        an aluminum armchair
        hung-up-on-some-roots—
                I love you

Human being
        turns its head
        to receive the beam
        thus delivered

and stores it away
in its earhouse

Philip, 1963
photo by E. Sottsass, Jr., Milano

Philip, Thos. Jackrell & Oscar Heiserman, Coach St., Portland 1963
photo by Allen Ginsberg,
Copyright Allen Ginsberg Trust

Jack Kerouac with Philip, 1956
photo by Walter Lehrman

Philip with Lloyd Reynolds in his living room, Portland 1963
photo by Allen Ginsberg,
Copyright Allen Ginsberg Trust

Philip at Ninnaji with Dr. & Mrs. Ch'en shih-hsiang, April 1966
photo by Gary Snyder

anne waldman
AFTER TU MU:
RECALLING FORMER TRAVELS #1

for Philip Whalen

lolled in
   meditation halls
bowed down to temple ground

gong it struck thus: gong gong gong

vernalization?

   keep talking about seeds

enlightenment DNA

or the vernix of mind

   blasphemy for the turn-coat world
& what gets quelled

   my waist my head my feet disappeared
in obeisance to mind

what is a little mind?

drollery
      kind linguistics
   respite from the very next thing

or mind is the very next thing

   rung on a ladder
a tongue a wag of which moves you
   to stop

reels of talk or celluloid

stop the queue of mind

   all lines being mind mind a quibble

then glim
  (his blue eye)

old memory: lantern
the night he arrived for steak dinner
   & it got burnt

phalansterian he might be

& never misread the body politic

on the lookout mountain

       mind went over the mountain
or mind jumped in the wooden cart

  prefer a synoptic account?

mind sat in a thousand places
drinking tea
writing thus as notation
of all that silken mind

  segments meant to swim

black silk like smooth naga skin
red silk that takes your breath away
  like seduction
yellow silk for Thailand

the silk road entered mind
mind entered civilization

when you walk you are not a rock
rock could be the corner of a tomb-civilization

mind, at least a bit of it, went into ink
ink came from mineral rock
went into branch

you stood gaping over the bone etcetera

awareness perception reasoning judgment

you stood drooling over the bone etcetera

awareness morphology steel cage frivolity

did you?

Japan: was it strict?

the sensible horizon
like an Horatian ode would never be
sung

tricking you
& come as conqueror to the point of an anvil
electromagnetic fields to a point of despair

can't hold all this in my mind, she "opined"

lyranx lyranx dear Philip
walking the prodigy world

  a mountain for your thought

glad we struck together

wasted no time
  climbing
 obscure being mind
 hills

making the poetry tree musculature

hills being mind wasted no time climbing

obscured

being mind inside the obscuring mind

get clear
or

salt the wound again

or get clear again

it is possible

saw the mountain world
wind around us

   Himalayas
    Andes
     Rockies

gave us being mind

  or never minded giving up the mind

to you

bow to you (many times)

"this bank and shoal of time"

(Naropa, circa 1984)

Philip at Beaver Street, 1965
© photo by Larry Keenan

Why do we need affection, if that isn't so much of what there is, as
essence, but the first time I sat at the kitchen table with you, in Chicago,
talking over cookbooks, it was the end of a long search for that kind of
friendship. But I had met you in Bolinas, and told you my brother was in
Vietnam, you'd drawn my cover, but that wasn't the same as. I can't talk
like this, it's in the air. It hurts to remember the letter I wrote from England,
asking you what love is. I was so distressed; and you told me it was what
transformed you, personal love, and made you — and you meant yourself
— capable, then, of going outwards towards others, the ones you didn't
know. Except you said something like, 'When I'm in love I like everybody on
the bus.' I remember you sitting, three months before he died, with Ted in
our New York apartment, you held the new cat and what I watched was
a calm transmission of affection between you two in your straight wood
chairs, at a time when Ted and I felt like pariahs, but that kind of commu-
nity judgment has never gotten near you. What we'd like is peace. A wish
that's never honored in the public world. The word meant a lot of things
at once, in the early 70's, who ever got it, even when the war was over,
because of what the Powers exact from us, but I think you might have any-
way. Peace, affection, motion in place — why did I say that? — emotion in
peace. All the times I've been with you. All the time we're in. There is noth-
ing cold about this light.

Philip on Ridge Trail, Mt. Tamalpais 1965
photo by John Whinham Doss, M.D.

Philip with a Michael McClure painting
© photo by Larry Keenan

dave haselwood
PHILIP MONTANUS

*"Whalen — a beautiful mountain
of flesh." Robert LaVigne*

I've come looking for you
In a place you've never been
    Yolla Bolly
    (snow-capped peak)
    a Wintun name
A wilderness,
Humble and remote
No Muir to glorify its name,
Its history an oral teaching still
From old men met on distant trails.

An invocation here on Soldiers Ridge
    —gray sandstone teeth and
    ancient wind shaped trees
And you appear,
Complaining of your feet,
To walk with me through
Knotted Jeffrey Pines
On rocky precipice and
Amber Incense Cedars
Rising from the astered earth
    ("You made that up," you say
    and give my ribs a dig.)

Now we have reached the meadow spring
Where we must choose between
Two trails
    Bear-savaged sign reads:
        <Solomon Peak
        French Cove>

And here we are again
Where we have always been,
Caught between wisdom's distant peak
And summer meadows far below.

<>

{Projector One}
We struggle up through slopes
Of scree and lichened jaggy rock,
Eyes focused just beyond our feet.
Epiphanies of perfect tiny flower
Set in barren crack; cramping muscle;
Sweat burned eye; cloud shadows;
Heaving chest.

Suddenly earth falls away and
All is just a fabric made of light
And shadow— cloudy shapes of
Airy mountain peaks.

<>

{Projector 2}
Down by shadowed trail
Fir forest scented tread
Of duff; by channeled seeps
Gathering to subtle sound
And lively air of
Falling mountain stream.

"Look IN," you said
As we walked into Arcady:
Green pasture for the prancing stag;
The Quail, his wife and all their progeny
Strolling beneath an acorn bearing oak;
And towering far above, gray Solomon
Is guardian of everything below.

<>

How quickly both projections fade!
How real they seemed!
The sign and rock lined spring,

The view toward Summit ridge,
Shine in fire of the westering sun.

You kneel among summer blooms and sedge,
Draw water from the sky-reflecting mystery.
I light the little stove and we make tea.
A mountain and a cove sit down to eat and drink,
To laugh and speak, a living breeze,
As evening turns to night.

> "Four times up, three times down?" I asked.
> "Just don't forget," you said,
> "Too much wisdom petrifies the flesh!"

We are on the mountain still.
<>
{Envoi}
"Great Master Quan of Daming monastery
Liked to write poetry and talk and laugh;
Master Heng tried to keep him in control.
But Master Quan just said,
'Human life is a dream.
Enjoying a lifetime is a good dream;
Keeping a life under wraps is a bad dream.
I would rather have a good dream.'"
(from *Case 90, The Book of Serenity*)

Yolla Bolly, August 2001

dave haselwood   53

clark coolidge
P.W.: SOME MEMORIES AND NOTIONS

During the furrowed brow sessions at Vancouver
he picks up a blue exam book by the door
fills it with loopy lines stray poems goofs and doodles
and hands it to the person who happens to be
sitting next to him when he leaves

The best reading I can remember
Philip musing publicly over his poems that Vancouver night
Monday in the Evening and "PLUSH" and Tennis shoes
and Minor Moralia the peak of his work but
not recorded since Olson said forget it
took Phil in chambers later told him
he didn't know how to register his lines
on the page no one is registered

Walked up behind Olson et al. on panel and wrote
a list of Gertrude Stein titles on the chalkboard
upstaging the discussion said
"You want to learn how to write read those"
and sat down

I first had Ted Berrigan and C "a great cuckoo magazine"
from his hands 1963

He showed what could be done
with a congeries of names nouns
irreducibles pockets thereof
a symphony of gems and eggs
solidities of the goof

He thought of just enough things to keep us all busy

The poet of breathable thought

7:II:01

Philip in Bolinas, 1968
photo by Zoe Brown

alastair johnston
FOR PHIL'S SAKE

Earlier in the interglacial age, there came from the North a Transcendental Triad: Gary Snyder, Lew Welch and Philip Whalen.

Whalen is a trickster, and a scholar, his erudition occasionally obscuring his wild sense of humour. Auerhahn Press published his first book, *Memoirs of an Interglacial Age* in 1960.

In 1969 Hardcore Basement published *On Bear's Head,* notable at the time because no one could afford is at $18, now recognised as one of the great visionary manuals of the post-War years.

Whalen, meanwhile, vamoosed to Japan. Becoming a Zen priest he forsook hirsute woodsiness for glabrous spirituality. A quasi-autobiographical trilogy appeared, naturally enough, as three novels, *You Didn't Even Try* (Coyote, 1967), *Imaginary Speeches for a Brazen Head* (Black Sparrow, 1972) and *The Diamond Noodle* (Poltroon, 1980). He is also the author of *Enough Said* (Grey Fox) & a cassette, *By & Large* (Ubik Sound).

He continues to be the most delightful and original poet of the interglacial epoch, and, as our favorite ad-man, Lew Welch said: "He cuts through grease, faster." Please welcome Philip Whalen.

* *
*

This was the introduction I made to a Whalen reading at Cody's about 1979. To it I must add my perpetual delight in hearing Phil read his work. His voices are a chorus of characters bickering inside his cranium, though each gets his or her moment in the mouthpiece.

I met Phil in 1974 when I was researching my bibliography of the Auerhahn Press, Dave Haselwood's San Francisco imprint that launched the careers of Whalen, Welch, Wieners and many others. Philip invited me to the Zen center on Page Street for tea and we chatted and got to know one another. Later I visited him in his home. I was impressed at how though he had no furniture, it was wonderfully furnished with displays of *suiseki* or "bonsaied" rocks (!) and Buddhist artifacts as well as the novel way his library was arranged, starting inside the door and running around the skirting board of the entire apartment on the floor. There were probably more books in the closets. He showed me portraits of himself done by McClure and Kerouac. I liked his own drawing better. He recommended *The Makioka Sisters* as a novel worth reading. I couldn't get into it, but I shared his taste for Jane Austen.

He showed me a book of Richard Brautigan's translated into Japanese and dedicated to him. He didn't know why Brautigan would dedicate a work to him, but it was clear to me. Brautigan was hot at the time, 1975 or so, and Phil was too modest to think he could have made an impact on the younger better-known poet's writing. Whalen was a big influence on the hippie generation and by far the best writer of his own generation, often dubbed the Beats. Eng Lit types think of Whalen, if they think at all, as a character in *The Dharma Bums* by Kerouac. (Kerouac is a character is *The Diamond Noodle*.) Yet Whalen was content to modestly sit in the background and be lumped with Welch and Snyder as part of some phenomenon arising out of Lloyd Reynold's calligraphy class at Reed College in Portland, Oregon.

As I had written a bibliography of Auerhahn and was very interested in his work, Phil started sending me notes and cards about some of his own early publications, thinking perhaps I'd do a bibliography of him. I was hired to design and typeset Gary Lepper's bibliography of *75 Modern American Authors* so was able to use some of this material to give Lepper an assist.

We'd go to lunch at Chinese restaurants. Sometimes Jim Nisbet would drive and the three of us would squeeze into the front of Jim's Datsun pickup. We were all thinner then. Phil loved to eat as well as talk. I often asked him for work to print and he always replied that he wasn't writing anymore. But then somehow Don Allen or another small press would bring something out, so I persisted and found manuscripts squirreled away in odd places which I was able to put into metal type as broadsides or the little book, *Prolegomena to a Study of the Universe* I did with an introduction by Kevin Power. Those prose pieces were later rewritten and incorporated into the text of *The Diamond Noodle*.

Don Allen had the manuscript of *The Diamond Noodle* and thought it was unpublishable. He willingly relinquished it to me. Somehow the original art that went with it had gotten detached from the manuscript and was considered lost. I asked Frances Butler to illustrate the book and she came up with some drawings that reacted to specific moments in the story. We showed them to Philip: he didn't like them. The drawings should have nothing whatever to do with the text, he said. That made it easy. We went through Frances' portfolio and selected a bunch of drawings she'd done for no specific goal (one a portrait of her mother, another of her late husband, two based on street photos by me) and showed them to Philip. He was happy, judged them the perfect accompaniment. But he had another request regarding the typesetting of the book: when he had written it, from 1956 to 1965 (pretty much concurrently with *On Bear's Head*), he had been partial to asterisks and had used pyramids of stars and asterisks to punctuate the layout. Whenever there was a break, instead of a number or chapter title, he had used stars. Lose them, he instructed me. I think he found that his typographic innovation had many followers from his earlier published work, and he was no longer eager to be part of the movement. I got rid of the stars but this caused problems in the paste-up and many imposition changes. I had set the book in photo-type so it was in long waxed galleys and not as easy to manipulate as digital or even metal type. It was the biggest project I had undertaken and I was still learning how it all fits together. But I knew enough not to try to impose too much external style on to the writing: rather to try to make the voice heard through subtle use of spacing, judicious use of italics and caps, and I followed his line breaks or indents as if it were a poetry manuscript. I had liked the stars, they were so, well, Whalenesque, and now there were gaps in the pages where they had been. I introduced large sizes of type—repros from metal Sabon—here and there, in lieu of chapter openings where there was an obvious new section, but my main contribution, typographically, was in creating two title-pages for imaginary books. I did them in early eighteenth-century English style which delighted him.

When the book was finished I sent back the manuscript and later found the pages of stars that were originally interspersed throughout. So I returned them separately. He sent me a long letter from Santa Fe detailing his itinerary whilst in San Francisco on a recent trip (as a way of excusing himself for not seeing me). He wrote (15 IX 87): "I hope you aren't *too* mad at me. Thanks for sending the lost pages of DIAMOND NOODLE {my stars!}. I'm

having fun reading Lord Byron's letters & journals. He was a sharp cookie."
He'd write little spontaneous poems as dedication in books I asked him to
sign, like "Onward, in search of the pheromone!" or

> Thanks for the procaine gases
> Welcome to Canada horses coffee
> Cup search. Realy nice. Who took it.

I loved getting letters and cards from him because of his wit and elegant
calligraphy. My favourite came in response to a copy of my magazine *The
Ampersand*. It reads:

> Dear Alastair, Thanks for sending
> the elegant magazine. I loved the
> "buncombe, balderdash & sham" article.
> Everything is creeping along at a
> petty pace, today and mostly mañana.
> I long for the fleshpots of Egypt &c.
> Hope you are all keeping well & happy.
> Yours &c
> Phil

12:VIII:86

At the end of the 80's he moved back to San Francisco from Santa Fe and
I visited him in his new Zendo which was above a laundromat on Portrero
Hill as I recall. I'd borrowed McClure's portrait of him for a show and it
was in really poor shape, being enamel paint on butcher paper. It was so
large he kept it rolled up in the closet and the ends were getting frayed. So
I took it to the top paper conservator in Oakland and had it restored and
de-acidified. He showed me his notebooks from his trip to Japan and since
he liked my work he gave me the original art for "Ten Titanic Etudes" and
a lot of similar poems from his Japan trip that were calligraphy and drawing
in bright multi-coloured felt pen. (The text is printed in *On Bear's Head*, pp.
377-79, but see the last pages of that volume as well as *Highgrade* for an
example of his drawn poems.) But he didn't really understand the printing
process: there was no way to reproduce work like this by letterpress and
offset-lithography would have cost a fortune. Iris prints were also out the
price range unless I wanted to make an artificial rarity and sell it for a lot

of money. But I held onto the pages hoping that as computer technology improved I might be able to scan them and print them on a color printer and gather them in a portfolio in a small edition. I asked Joanne Kyger to write an introduction, which she did, and I set it in type, and designed a title page using large wood type but went no further. (Finally an archival Epson printer is coming onto the market as I write this, in July 2002).

* *
*

Once Phil told me of the time he was making a pilgrimage in Japan. He was headed for a remote monastery with a friend. As they approached the village where the monastery was situated they thought to bring a gift and stopped into the village store. There wasn't much available, and their Japanese was rudimentary, and so they decided a practical gift would be a bottle of sake. So they asked for sake. Unfortunately the store only had it in 5 gallon jugs. Well, they thought, it could be appreciated as the monastery could stock up. They reached the monastery, lugging the huge jeroboam of liquor, and duly presented their gift to the abbot. Later they were invited to dinner and when they arrived in the candle-lit dining hall, the monks came out in procession bearing trays with hundreds of tiny cups all full of the sake which they laid on the table before the pilgrims!

Allen Ginsberg and Philip upon the occasion of the circumnabulation of Mt. Tamalpais, on the festival of Buddha's birthday,
April 8, 1968
photo by R.J. Greensfelder

Philip and Allen Ginsberg, San Francisco, September 1971
photo by Gordon Ball

Philip and Allen Ginsberg at Naropa, 1975
photo from Rocky Mountain News

61

diane diprima
TO PHILIP WHALEN, 1999

I THREW IT OUT

all the typesetting I did of
"On Bears Head"   for
Poets Press
                (it took me 2 yrs
                to do it)

Threw it out. I was so mad.
you chose
                Big Press &
                $1500 over
                us.

Wish now I'd kept it.
At least it had
                        all yr little
                        Squiggles &
                        drawings

painstaking pasted in.
                        right into the poems
                        like you had em

Only today, 32 yrs later &
reaching for that book to show a student

I notice
the Big Press in NYC
left nearly all of them
                        OUT

wish now
I had that paste-up

gone

in a trash can
in Millbrook

I was so mad.

L-R top: Jerry Heiserman, Dan McCloud, Allen Ginsberg, Bobbie Louise Hawkins Creeley, Professor Warren Tallman (slightly above right), Robert Creeley
L-R bottom: Thomas Jackrell, Philip Whalen, Don Allen and Charles Olson (with crossed legs)
Vancouver Poetry Conference, July 1963.
Copyright Allen Ginsberg Trust

michael mcclure
FLOWER GARLAND FROTH—
for Zenshin Ryufu, Philip Whalen

THROUGH THE SKANDHAS, THE BUNDLES

OF BRIGHTNESS AND HUNGERS,

arises

more FOAM

making foam with no origin

but mutual reflection

Taste   hunger   perception   thought

NO

JOKE

not even traps

gorgeous manacles

((physical form-bubbles

sensation-bubbles

perception-bubbles

conditioning-bubbles

consciousness-bubbles

<<>>

MALLARME'S HUGE PASSIONS AND

FRANCESCO CLEMENTE'S

tiny, skinny dark figures in the joy of their excrement

and bright excitement, and Blake's fairies

and caterpillars

swimming in nada, right where we breathe

The Circus of Celebration runs away

with us

(not us with the circus!)

pulling us out of the big top

like kernels from

a wrinkled shell

more foam

FOAM POPPING BY THE SIDE OF THE RIVER

rainbow bubbles burst, while reflecting all
                                        things

from a black smooth rock

made of bubbles

A white hand

reaches

TO FILL A VASE

from the cool stream

Bronze vase clinks

on a stone

foam

More foam

<<>>

FOAM WHERE A SKUNK DRINKS

from the trickle   elegant black and white

fur of foam

Sound of the water

foam   bubbles

FUR

OF

A

MOVING TRUCK

michael mcclure   67

in the wet forest   Paint chips

on mulch

A huge presence and purpose

bursting into being

with everything

Solid nothing

<<>>

... SOLID FOAM-BUBBLES BURSTING

INTO OLD SHOES   NEW SHOES

black with high tops

bubbles of irridescent soil on

the soles

Smell of redwood and wet mulch

in countless realms of

reflections

IN

JUST

one body

or none

trickling over the mirror

<<>>

HERE IS THE TRUE CONTENT OF EXPERIENCE

THE UNTRUE CONTENT OF EXPERIENCE

silver raindrops falling on bubbles

Words spill from sleep

Hungry ghosts behind trees

push over dreams   NOT

TRUE

Tiny black seeds

rattle in an envelope

BIG SCARLET FLOWERS

Bubbles

Foam

<<>>

A SWORD WITH EDGES OF FLAME

slashes the walls

BLACK ANTS CIRCLE A BUBBLE OF HONEY

Zerbras, wildebeest,

at the waterhole

Smell of red dust in the air

is foam

Uncoiling fiddle-neck ferns,

astroturf,

voices of wisdom

BLADE THROUGH A RAINBOW MEMBRANE

<<>>

EVERYTHING SMILING

with haloes and imaginary radiance

ALL FOAM

real

as delusion

and the sunyatta physics of pond plants

and hot air ducts

blowing into outburstings

of snow banks

These caves

are inhabited by nothings constructed

of bubbles

I drive them around

and eat them

<<>>

FALCON SHAPES WOVEN IN GRAY SILK

Tension of plum buds

in night fog

Stars a trillion years

from the mist

BUBBLES

all in one

ONE

IN ALL

Hidden in moss

in the redwoods

near a Butterfinger wrapper

<<>>

THE SOUND OF THE DOWNPOUR ON WALLS

is bubbles bursting

into stuff of delusion,

fine as a new chip on an old tooth

LIKE

THE TECHNICOLOR MOVIE

of smells projected between raindrops

on a screen of touches and tastes

The message of flannel is foam

for the shoulders

in the perfume

while floorboards shine

Perfectly clear

<<>>

I RISE PROUD TO BE BEING

michael mcclure   73

as

I

am

and I

lie

silent

NOT

KNOWING

I

Know

I

know

the long-gone delicacy

and meat of apricots

sun-heated on branches,

and waves and caverns of fuel

smashing the earth

in the arising

and pouring

of patterns

I love those who fight this

I

HAND

THEM

the primate crown

shimmering

with hunger and automobiles

and velvet and contracts and postage

and duck weed and emeralds

and jazz

THIS IS NOT MINE

THIS WILL NOT BE MINE

THIS IS NOT MINE

THIS WILL NOT BE MINE

This is not mind

This will not be mind

THIS IS NO BODY

THIS WILL NOT BE BODY

.

Me

is

not

mine

It appears on the tip of an eyelash

A bubble

Foam

For the twenty-fifth anniversary of the ordination of Philip Whalen

Philip and Michael McClure, May 1980
photo by Peter Holland

Philip and Michael McClure, March 1989
photo by Leslie Scalapino

norman fischer
ALONG THE LINES OF PHILIP WHALEN

At home the vegetable supply

Along the trailing edge

Of life is the only fit subject

Broad-rim soup dish BLASH

Out there the garbage needs to

BLASH Daitokuji monastery

Churchbells ring over every hand and face

Here at the edge of town people visit me

We've got to have amusement

Lets go in lets go in deeper

Work, every day, no time to feel sad and friendless

Or have we proven that. We take

(Rapeseed oil, waterproof paper umbrella)

We really deserve progression not indigestion

The plum tree functions gorgeously

Let's not go forward at all

Philip at San Francisco Zen Center, Page St., December 26, 1980
photo by Arthur Winfield Knight

david schneider

1 Oct 1981

Brian knocked at my door and stood there sweating, irritated, incredulous that John and I could be so irresponsible as to be late for a meeting. "God, it makes me mad. I got a schedule you know . . . "
"OK, where's John?"
"I don't know, I thought I'd find him here."
"Well, why don't you look downstairs, or in the courtyard?"
"It really pisses me off, you know."

While Brian was gone I finished cleaning up the calligraphy gear, and there came a loud knock on the door, the kind a couple of cops might use before they rushed in to bust you "BLAM BLAM BLAM. . ." Hello, Hello? Anybody in there? Hello? BLAM BLAM.
It could only be Philip.
"Hello, Hello," I yelled as I opened the door.
"Hello, Hello," he continued, looking at me. "Is that you? Hello? You've got to invite us (PW and Michael Wenger) in now, for tea and cookies and charming conversation."
"You can certainly come in, but I don't have any tea here, or any hot water..."
"We don't want any of your goddamn excuses, we want tea!" They traipsed in, having removed their shoes. "Besides, we brought you gorgeous art to look at."
Philip handed me an enormous pad of Bristol board, from which he'd used sheets to copy out a section of *Scenes of Life at the Capitol*. The fragment he'd copied was about *Jizo bodhisattva;* it was his part of our joint effort to do another broadside - poetry and Siddham calligraphy, handprinted on nice paper, limited edition. The commercial purpose for this poster was to raise

funds for Zen Center's purchase of a Jizo figure.

I set the pad on the floor, and leafed through until I found his handwriting. The poem was fit into the central third of a large sheet, written carefully in a tight, Italic hand. It looked great. "I fucked up a little at the end," he said. It was true. At the very bottom of the poem, where he was telling that he'd copied it out at the South Ridge Zendo, he'd left the 'd' out of 'Ridge.' With a carat, he'd indicated where the missing 'd' should go, and written one. I didn't think it mattered much, but I could imagine how he'd cursed when he'd discovered the mistake.
"I got carried away in the excess of glorious achievement, I guess."

Brian came back, doubly mad, because John was nowhere. He steamed into the room, and was all set to blow up when he noticed that we were sitting around this lovely poem, this lovely handwriting, and were under its influence. He began to read it.
"That's really beautiful," he said, eyes big and round and calm. "What's it for?"

5 Oct. 81

Philip and I had planned to take our calligraphy over to Peter and Shelly Koch's Black Stone Press as early as we could get free. I stacked my originals, Philip's originals, some reductions of the syllables and some art books into a cloth, packed it all up, and drove a borrowed van over to Phil's. I got there about 9:45 am, and even though I'd eaten breakfast, I was somehow shaking with hunger, fatigue, coffee nerves, and driving nerves by the time I got to his door.
"How are you?"
"I've got the shakes, actually. Do you have something small to munch on?"
"Certainly. Come in and start on this tea." He poured me the last cold cup of a teapot. I drank some of it and could feel little knots forming up around where the shoulders met my neck.
"You want some bread—I got some bread here. You want some bread and butter?"
"That sounds wonderful."
He handed me the food and I rummaged in his neat kitchen for a knife and found one finally. Philip stood with one hand on the refrigerator door, holding it open, and spoke into the fridge, as if addressing a group of people in

there. He called out a list. "You want eggs? I got eggs; milk? Horseradish? Pickles? I'm out of cheese. Cucumber? Po-ta-to?"

As soon as my mouth wasn't too full, I answered, "This is fine, really."

He kept on: "Mayonnaise? Lettuce, tomato. . ." I took a cherry tomato, and he stopped long enough to advise me that they were no good. "Olives, ketchup, onion, lemon?"

Eventually we got ourselves strapped into the van, and over to the Black Stone Press. Peter lives with his pretty and talented wife Shelly, a 3-year old son called Max, and a dog, in a giant old warehouse. It's in a rough part of the Mission District—they want to move—but they've got it fixed up wonderfully, with the front half for all the hand presses, paper cutters, type cabinets and flat files and the back half, separated by a kind of stretched-cloth fence, made into vast living quarters.

Peter greeted us and as usual we talked about everything else in the world but printing—or at least this particular job—for about 15 or 20 minutes. Finally we got to work, trying to lay out the art so Peter could get a couple of zinc plates made. This was not easy as there were 7 or 8 separate slippery pieces of writing, and all of us were of the "eyeball" school of design. We nearly went blind trying to get a decent balance of elements.

We set the work on a table, and roughed out where things should go. We'd take turns standing on a chair, squinting at the effect, climbing down to move this or that part a bit, then climbing back up to squint at it again. Philip only went for the climbing bit at first. He decided to let me do the scampering and sat instead looking at various pretty things Peter kept showing him—this book, that printed poem, such and such a newsletter.

I said, "THERE, that's good. I think. Phil, you come look."

"Well," he said from his perch, after he stopped grunting from the effort of climbing, "Well, Dave," putting his hand on my shoulder for support, "I think I'd like that part down just a cunt hair more, or so. I dunno. . . "

At one point we put it all on the floor, to avoid the chair business, but the little dog forced us back up to a safer altitude, with his stray hairs and lolling tongue.

We argued about white space: Philip wanted tons, like in the Tara broadside; I wanted tons too, but I didn't just want a bunch of parts floating. I thought it all had to hold together somehow and be enclosed by the edges of the paper. I told him that the only complaint anyone at all had had about the Tara print was that it was a little too big.

"Goddamn people just don't know any better is all. It's the same damn thing as when Dave Haselwood printed my *Memoirs of an Inter-Glacial Age*. He ran it up on that Italian paper, with lots of white space, so that it was this beautiful THING, you know. And everybody came and complained that it wouldn't fit in their bookshelves because it was oversize. Goddamn rubes didn't know what they were getting! Well, some people knew; some could see they were getting lots of yummy paper, and they bought them all up. That and anything else Dave Haselwood did when he was with Auernhahn Press. Gorgeous things."

Peter the younger printer nodded his head solemnly during this speech. I just stood on the chair and continued squinting at parts and fussing with them. We tried different size sheets of paper; we tried different orientations of the paper, I really liked the smaller sizes better, yummy paper or not. "Well Marc Davidson, I'll tell you what," Philip began in very slow tones, as if making a great concession, as if he were a plantation owner or some-thing, about to set the slaves free. "I'll come down as far as THIS sheet, in terms of the side margins . . . BUT! . . . I have to have at least THIS much vertical space. I have to. I require it."

I felt fine about that. I was mostly worried that things were floating out to the sides in any case, and of course we needed space at the bottom, to write signatures and doodle or whatever and to place chops. I was all for it. Especially as I was feeling faint, and hungry again as usual. I wanted to be gone.
We talked fairly quickly about which kind of high-class paper to print, and went along with Peter's first suggestion. After a few solemn warnings to him about not moving to Bolinas—no water, too many sociable people, rural slum, (Phil kept saying how hard it was to "haul groceries in there") —we took our leave.

Philip in San Francisco, 1977
photo by Phiz Mezey

andrew schelling
PHILIP WHALEN'S DHARMA ROAR

This portrait was written at the behest of Helen Tworkov, editor of Tricycle: The Buddhist Journal. *It appeared in an abridged version in 1993. Most of the quotes by Whalen come from an interview conducted in Philip's Hartford Street Zen Center quarters by Anne Waldman and myself on September 16, 1991. The interview appeared in* GAS, *in abridged form in the* Shambala Sun, *and finally in* Disembodied Poetics: Annals of the Jack Kerouac School *(University of New Mexico Press, 1994).*

On Saturday September 14, 1991, the American poet Philip Whalen, known also by his Buddhist name Zenshin Ryufu, was installed Abbot of the Hartford Street Zen Center in San Francisco. An assembly comprised of Zen practitioners in black robes, ranking arhats and bodhisattvas from both Zen and Vajrayana Buddhist traditions, poets in blue jeans and boots, long-time friends, local chroniclers, disciples, hearers, kinnaras, gnomes, nautch girls, serpents, demons, and attendants from Hartford Street's attached AIDS hospice, were present for the ceremony in the basement meditation hall. Zenshin formally accepted the Abbot's seat, staff, and horse-fly whisk with the words, "The seat is empty. There is no one sitting in it. Please take good care of yourselves."

As a Buddhist teacher Philip Whalen holds a subdued profile, serving more as an example to a few fellow practitioners than as a formal instructor. It was not until 1987 that he left his own teacher, Baker-roshi, who in Whalen's brisk telling of it said, "Alright, go away—go away and do something, go away and do your own thing. Good bye."

It would seem that Whalen's "thing" is to sit, to sit early and late, to open the zendo at Hartford Street, ring the bells, perform bows and ceremonial functions, and otherwise go about the quiet work of naturalizing Buddhism to American soil. He insists on practice and regards it as the specific imperative for American Zen. "As far as meditation is concerned," he said at a Green Gulch Zen Center conference in 1987, "I'm a professional. I've been a professional since 1973. And that's my job. I find it very difficult to sell." He has no books of Dharma talks, few students, and avoids the circuit of Buddhist teachers and institutions.

What then are his teachings? How does one locate them? I would urge every halfway literate person in this country towards Philip's books of poetry. Though he won't acknowledge them as teaching devices, resisting the suggestion that they embody contemplative states of mind, they are packed with that strict wild Zen humor, enough to make the buddhas of old slap their thighs. In conversation and in Dharma talks Whalen invokes Gertrude Stein, who insisted that writing is "Beginning again and again, always beginning again,"—which conjures both the spontaneous mind-awareness practice of contemporary American poets, and Suzuki Roshi's ancient *Beginner's Mind*. Writing has been Whalen's long-held passion. "Jack Kerouac said that writing is a habit like taking dope. Well I have a writing habit, and I have a sitting habit." And though many who know Whalen's writings or reputation have come to them through his legendary friendship with better known colleagues like Kerouac, the lineage he belongs to is ancient and precise.

Hymnus Ad Patrem Sinensis

I praise those ancient Chinamen
Who left me a few words,
Usually a pointless joke or a silly question
A line of poetry drunkenly scrawled on the margin of a quick
            splashed picture—bug, leaf,
            caricature of Teacher
        on paper held together now by little more than ink
        & their own strength brushed momentarily over it

Their world and several others since
Gone to hell in a handbasket, they knew it—
Cheered as it whizzed by—
& conked out among the busted spring rain cherryblossom winejars
Happy to have saved us all.

                                    31:viii:58

Celebrating impermanence with tough humor. Compassion that has no truck with sentimentality. Whalen learnt his art at the feet of monks, hermits and word-wizards who still delight us. In India, the originally oral *gathas* (songs) gathered in the *Theragatha* and *Therigatha,* sung by disciples of the excellent Buddha himself. In the Orient, Han Shan, Li Po and Tu Fu, Lady Komachi, Hakuin Zenji, Murasaki Shikibu and Basho. On our North American landmass, Kenneth Rexroth, Gertrude Stein, Thomas Wolfe, Jack Kerouac. Do not think of this stuff as religious poetry! These are the crafted gestures in language that define whole civilizations—that transmit to people such imperatives as how to laugh, when to grieve, where to observe a flower or a watershed, how to place oneself in history, even how to free oneself of the notion of a permanent Self. These teachings, available through friends, teachers and poetry, survive the collapse of every civilization. Within this international, multi-millennial avant-garde Philip Whalen's poetry has worked out its tender unpredictable directives.

Born in Portland, Oregon, in 1923, then raised in The Dalles, a little town set along a narrows of the Columbia River, Whalen was drafted during World War II into the U.S. Army Air Corps as a radio operator. As he tells it in a succession of interviews collected in the Four Seasons Foundation book *Off the Wall,* he spent several years lying in the glass-bottomed hull of a fighter-bomber, hurtling over the California deserts, reading the books of Thomas Wolfe and imagining that, could he himself write novels like those, he might achieve fame and riches. A friend, one of those disguised Bodhisattvas that throw the most useful obstacles in our paths, saved us all from a shelf of such epics by placing in Whalen's hand a book of Gertrude Stein's, which splendidly diverted him into the discoveries of twentieth century modernism.

After the War, out of money and wanting time to write, Whalen signed up for college under the G.I. Bill. He returned to the Northwest in 1946 to attend Reed College in Portland, spending his government checks on books and staying home to read. By this time considering himself a poet, he took a house with Lew Welch and Gary Snyder. Snyder recalls that the first practicing poet he met was Philip Whalen. Whalen had also since high school been studying Hindu texts and investigating a variety of Asian traditions. Where did the Zen come from?

> Important landmarks might begin with Gary Snyder discovering R.H. Blyth's four volume set of haiku translations that came out in the fifties. Blyth keeps referring to Suzuki Daisetz in his notes... That's how Gary got to looking up the *Essays in Zen Buddhism.* So we read all those, Suzuki's three volumes, and a bunch of other material, but it pretty much started with the haiku translations.

Lloyd Reynolds, one of Whalen and Snyder's literature teachers at Reed, held a passion for Western-style calligraphy based on a sixteenth century Italian model. He was simultaneously reawakening the art of Western calligraphy and training his Reed College students to work with pen and ink. Whalen began to fill up notebooks in his own distinct hand, doodling and drawing his way into poems like an Oriental painter-poet, each word an exercise in attention as he moved the nib of a calligraphy pen—a practice that seems to be his own distinct contribution to Buddhist practice and spontaneous prosody. Over the years he's pieced together massive layered poems from these quick humorous notebook pages—pages that resemble

Hakuin Zenji's irreverent poem-scrawls, or the illuminated manuscript of some whiskey-mad Irish monk. Several of Whalen's books reproduce these pages—words inseparable from the gestures that freed them.

> A line of poetry drunkenly scrawled on the margin of a quick
> splashed picture—bug, leaf,
> caricature of Teacher.

College finished, Whalen drifted down the coast to San Francisco along with his friends, writing his tough, funny, extraordinarily learned verse and working odd jobs, including a series of summers for the Forest Service back in the Northwest. Along the way he met and befriended other poets and contemplatives—Allen Ginsberg, Jack Kerouac, Kennth Rexroth —joining them for the legendary reading at the Six Gallery in 1955 where Ginsberg first read "Howl" and an excitable Kerouac passed the hat for wine. He divided his next eighteen years between Japan and San Francisco, teaching English to Japanese students, studying Zen, writing copiously, seeing many books of poetry and two novels into print—and sitting. In Japan he observed Zen monks practicing their traditional way—the vows, the fierce good-humored work, the ungarnished ceremony. Their discipline attracted him.

> Zen seemed to cut away many extravagances and get down to the point of emancipation and energy and cutting loose from all your emotional problems. Everything that used to hang you up goes away or at least you can deal with it in some other way...In Zen there is a great deal to understand—the long historical tradition, the connections with the various sutras and so forth—but the Zen experience cannot be explained, you have to be it, you have to practice it.

When Philip returned for good to North America, Richard Baker-roshi, a senior student and Dharma heir of Suzuki Roshi, formally accepted him as a student. Whalen received the Buddhist name Zenshin Ryufu, and on February 3, 1973 at San Francisco Zen Center, Baker-roshi ordained him *Unsui,* Zen Buddhist Monk.

Whalen's cranky, intimate, wise poetry draws freely on the old Zen tradition, rooted in India and China, never indulgent, constantly testing its own limits. Don't search among his works for any of that posturing so often palmed off as Zen-inspired haiku. Grown on American soil, salted with local vernacular, his poems transmit the sharp Zen flash that gave the world such verse as Basho's. Here is Whalen, big as Basho with humor and affection towards the planets little sentient beings.

Ginkakuji Michi

Morning haunted by the black dragonfly
        landlady pestering the garden moss

10:v:66

Whalen is also one of the most widely read, subtly learned persons
around. Without losing the bite of American speech patterns, he seasons
his poetry with foreign phrases, Chinese ideograms, sharp philosophical
jokes, allusions to classics East and West. Poets and philosophers, historians,
satirists, emperors and ladies stride through his verse. He fusses and pleads
with a succession of muses, candidly studies the habits of elderly women,
pens scandalous letters to poets of his own generation, toys with imaginary
beasts, and upbraids the many Bodhisattvas for their self-satisfaction and
smug foolishness.

From the time of its North American popularization as a kind of
goofy instigator of Beat Generation writing in the 1950s, Zen in America
has struggled with charges of anti-intellectualism. These are not wholly
unearned. There exists a disciplined and ferocious humor that outwardly
appears contemptuous of words, dismissive of book learning, exasperated
with plodding scholarship, and disdainful of "the stink of religion." Tough
as it is on those addicted to book learning, Zen is a tradition that endlessly
refreshes itself with the written word. Since those distant Shaolin Temple
days when Bodhidharma wrote down his discoveries about "wall gazing,"
poem and anecdote, sutra and folksong, even learned commentary, have
been central to its teachings and transmission. Skillful poets hidden in robes
or rags have wandered its hallways, leaving precious rhymes which teachers
use to hone the insight of students.

So do poets keep company with demons, as the Japanese poet
Ikkyu playfully charged? Is the passion for language a devious snare? What
can you get out of books? Only the over-sophisticated could miss Whalen's
impeccable answer, given in Dharma combat to William Butler Yeats.

Homage to WBY

after you read all them books
all that history and philosophy and things
what do you know that you didn't know before?

Thin sheets of gold with bright enameling

23:xi:63

Aside from the black ink and red herrings scattered through his own books, the only solid literary portrait of Philip Whalen I can find occurs in Kerouac's *Desolation Angels,* and in *Big Sur,* that poignant account of Kerouac's alcohol breakdown. Unique among the raging poets, reckless travelers, suicidal girls, tough women, and down and out hobos that populate Kerouac's books, Whalen may be the solitary Bodhisattva sketched in language. A portly, sweet poet, he goes by the name Ben Fagan. In one passage, Kerouac caught in the throes of alcoholic derangement passes out in a San Francisco park. Ben Fagan calmly seats himself in lotus position on the grass to watch over his helpless companion. Six hours later when the narrator wakes up, his angelic guardian smiles at him, having not shifted posture. Not the amphetamine, sex and automobile stuff you build culture heroes for young readers out of. No. A portrait, rather, that edges towards that calm robed figure in a *thangka* painting, standing among a host of consumptive ghosts, who extends a gentle almost mockingly tender finger towards the blank round enlightenment moon.

One of Whalen's notable books is titled *Heavy Breathing*—actually a collection of three smaller books of cranky Zen inspired poetry. The "caricature of Teacher," some baffled little Bodhidharma that floats on the bright orange cover, neatly depicts a groundless, contemplative life. Yet why "Heavy Breathing?" What sort of title is that?

It is a first stipulation in the meditation hall that one breathe lightly, with minimal commotion. In courtesy to one's fellow creatures who are assiduously working out their salvation on cushions alongside you, one simply does not gasp or emit audible sighs. Yet historical circumstances have at times demanded a contravening of rules. An example: in June of 1963, after lengthy consideration, several Vietnamese monks transgressed the Buddhist stricture against suicide, and immolated themselves in Saigon before a gang of newsmen. In an out-of-hand political situation they made themselves human torches—to bring an urgent message to a world grown numb through TV addiction. Whalen's poetry—less dramatic since words being made out of breath are less dramatic—arrives as a deliberate disturbance in the shrine room—knocking the statues over, feeding the offerings to a hungry child—or even more disruptive, breathing heavily as though something's the matter.

> If Socrates and Plato and Diotima
> And all the rest of the folk at that party
> Had simply eaten lots of food and wine and dope
> And spent the entire weekend in bed together
> Perhaps Western Civilization
> Wouldn't have been such a failure?

The point is, we live now in a World-as-Zendo. History is our knottedly difficult *koan*. Hence practices unlike those associated with Zen centers in the past have arisen—Hartford Street's AIDS hospice an exemplary one. It arose very simply out of the recognition that people in the Center's Noe Valley neighborhood were dying painfully, and the San Francisco hospitals held insufficient beds.

But the history of Zen, which enshrines in its folklore numberless accounts of unprecedented behavior, also insists that such outbursts proceed from a condition of impeccable discipline. Whalen in a similar spirit champions his writer friends—the people, rigorously disciplined in their writing practices, whose job it is to get a little outrageous and disrupt things. Whalen speaks tenderly of Jack Kerouac, on a note strikingly different from Kerouac's media image. "His novels are very carefully composed, they weren't simply rattled off a typewriter the way the critics in New York said. His books are the result of immense attention, of an immense training, years of practice... it's a real art, it isn't simply a mishmash thrown together."

Taking stock of fellow writers like Kerouac, Whalen has noted the appearance in America, since the days of Thoreau and Emerson, of the "erratic practitioner." They are *erratics,* he says—citing a technical term for those huge puzzling rocks left behind aeons ago when a glacier passed through. And Whalen speaks of friend and fellow poet Lew Welch, who vanished into the forests of California in May, 1971. Welch would practice zazen on an immense rock off the shore of Muir Beach, or load a typewriter and a bundle of books into his rucksack and strike off into the mountains in search of a remote cabin, to meditate, study and write. "That sort of individual, hermit, erratic practice, is something that's really important. The danger of Zen Centers or monasteries is that people will take them seriously as being real. We should find out our own practice," Whalen says. "We might start out in an official place, but we should discover somehow that we don't need official institutions."

That's the thorny contemplative speaking, who needs no more than a reed mat to sit on. It's the poet speaking as well. There exists a luminous body poets inhabit—a body of words, free as the buddhas of old—in which they pass though the world. In *Big Sur* Kerouac left this portrait—

> There he sits cross-legged, leaning slightly to the left, flying softly through the night with a Mount Malaya smile. He appears as a blue mist in the huts of poets five thousand miles away. He's a strange mystic living alone smiling over books...

Issan Dorsey and Philip, Santa Fe, November 1986
photo by Mary Holm

Philip with Zentatsu Richard Baker at Tassajara
after the Hossenshiki Ceremony, November 1975
photo by Ted Howell

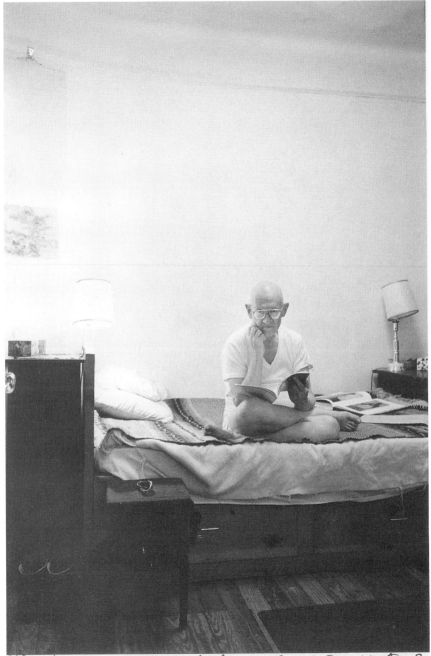

Philip Whalen Sensei visiting New York from Santa Fé Zen Center read poetry & lectured for Brooklyn College Lit. Hist. Beat Gen. Class a few days earlier, now resting in the bedroom my apartment Lower East Side Manhattan March 16, 1987. for Phil ~ Allen Ginsberg

Philip in San Francisco, early 1981
photo by Christopher Felver

miriam sagan
CONTENTMENT

Woke up to the finches crowing
Peaked into a nest, male and female sitting together
Looking out with sleepy beady finch eyes
Not like waking up 2 AM
Thinking of Frank dying in New York City
And angry at everyone because dying is so expensive
Last night driving up Cerro Gordo road
I remembered how I'd forgotten New Mexico again and again
And the foothills lay like little girls on their sides
Covered in scrub and snow.
Stars out and all the unidentified shining objects:
Planets, planes, space shuttle debris
Halley's comet, handmirror, handmaiden,
A pool of water—star bathing
Star as a woman—healing water—
Ojo Caliente—she keeps glowing—
Long haired angel of midnight not of morning—
Easy—this girl for wooing—
Song—spiral—downward—maze for threading—
Labyrinth—the body's cunt and asshole—
Knife in hand and star arising
Over island, desert, fall-out
Watershed, in helium brewing
All things simultaneous
Over the little park
Over the road of dirt
Over the rim of the world

Over the blue of the wide
Over the before and after
Over the call and laughter
The universe, contented in its curve.
Philip, fat zen priest, bald head, old, perfect, cranky
Playing baroque music on the Casio keyboard
And the cat Lily illegally and happily curled on his blanket
Room like a curio shop in San Francisco Chinatown
Long crystals, fossils, Buddhas, odd blue deities
And a white ceramic Bodhisattva
With an unconvincing number of arms
And Philip told me "you can ring the bells"
And I rang this long strand of metal cowbells from Tibet
That sounded like Pema the thanka painter's hand clasp
Felt warm and green/brown in high up country.
Once Pema showed me a picture
"This is my uncle's horse," he said
In a tone of such happiness
At being related to everybody.
Philip's room fills me with greed
And a sense that we are going to die
Greed because he will probably die before I do
And then I will get the chance to have something of his.
What I meant to say...
What I meant to say is...
What I meant...
That time my favorite finch died
I ran into the kitchen crying and said to Philip and my husband
Promise you won't die, ever!
And Philip said: I'm afraid you got to us a little too late for that.

SOUTH RIDGE ZENDO

Walking to Philip's downhill in the rain
A bird embryo on the sidewalk
Zazen organizes events around itself
Like opening or closing a green umbrella.

Tears begin when I sit with incense
Like the smell of you late last night
Hair full of smoke and earth
As you pull my pants off in bed.

Bowing together now
An unopened rosebud on the altar.
Outside in raindrops we can't stop laughing
Did you see Philip pull that thread out of his robe?

Mindless, happy, going home I am singing
All Buddhas, ten directions, three times
I've Got A Right To Sing The Blues and
Buddy Can You Spare A Dime.

Climbing uphill, an almost full moon
Hits me like a moan in the belly
And I turn to look and *see*
White bell flowers heavy on the stem.

Phil Whalen did not like New Mexico, an antipathy he did not attempt to hide. It reminded him too much of the eastern Oregon of his youth—dry, mountainous, and boring. It was following the Dharma path which brought him to Santa Fe in 1984, where his teacher Baker-roshi had relocated. Whalen lived in New Mexico off and on throughout the eighties. Like many things in life, the desert both amused and irked him. He missed the ocean, and once gave a Zen lecture about "a golden land, a paradise to the West," which to his listeners' amazement turned out not to be some Buddha realm but the city of San Francisco, complete with references to specific Chinatown dim sum parlors. He'd been born in a dry place, and moaned that didn't want to die in one. Still, he was hardly insensitive to the beauty of a sunset over the Cerro Gordo Park or the sight of a great blue heron rustling out of a dead tree at Bosque del Apache.

I met Phil through my husband, the late Robert Winson, who as a fellow Zen student and lover of poetry, followed Whalen around for several years, and in the process took him grocery shopping, cooked him blini with caviar, and drove him around New Mexico. I was afraid of Philip Whalen at first–enormous, opinionated, given to loud declamations—but I soon grew to love him. The first conversation I ever had with him was folding sheets at the laundromat on Water Street, where he lectured me on Jacobean drama while holding one edge of a sheet. He took dainty dancing steps backward and forward as he folded and declaimed.

Philip needed to be entertained, which in his case often meant lunch. He usually insisted on red meat, which couldn't be cooked in the Zen temple. So off we went to Mr. Steak where patrons often stared at us. Robert sported a long pronged Hassidic beard in those days, I favored earrings in the shape of plastic fruit, but really it was Phil who drew the stares, clad as he often was in a large white T-shirt and a day-glo orange hat. Once in the Army Navy surplus store a young man came up to Phil who was attired as usual with the addition of his *rakasu* and said: "Sir, I don't know exactly what you do but I know it is *something* and I want to follow you."

I often had the same vague feeling about Phil. I was convinced he was about to reveal the secret of poetry to me. I'd give him long poems I'd written and he'd mark the lines he hated with little renditions of a skull and crossbones. Once when I was devastated by the continuing rejection of my first novel I was lying on the carpet of our scantily furnished apartment on West San Francisco Street when Phil came in the door and stepped over my prone body. "I would not add alcohol to this situation if I were you, Miriam," he intoned–perhaps the only literary advice he ever gave me.

He did on occasion give me other advice. Once when I was complaining about having cramps Phil said: "do you know what Virginia Woolf's mother used to tell her when she had cramps?"

"What?" I asked, feeling confused about whether Virginia Woolf had a mother.

"Eat artichoke bottoms," Phil said. So I did.

Phil liked to watch Dr. Who, which was shown on Saturday nights on PBS. So off we went religiously to view the cheesy BBC science fiction series with him.

"They have spared no expense!" he always exclaimed, as actors trooped about in costumes obviously borrowed off the back lot of another production. Once he startled and intrigued me by looking with loathing at a hideous garish ashtray resting on a coffee table and yelling: "Will somebody turn that God damn ashtray down!" Phil and I did share something, I realized, we were both apt to go into sensory overload even from something as innocuous as an ashtray.

The poems Phil wrote in New Mexico had an ephemeral off-the-cuff feeling to them. They were recently collected in *Some of These Days* (Desert Rose Press, 1999). The poems read like cut-ups, with lines that sound like snatches of internal dialogue merged with bits of the overheard, and they bring Phil's speaking voice back to me: "The development of insight consumes great quantities of protein" and "I love Arizona but there isn't any seafood there."

Miriam Sagan, Robert Winson, Suzi Winson and Philip Whalen
Cerro Gordo Temple, Santa Fe, 1985
photo by permission of Suzi Winson

robert winson
from DIRTY LAUNDRY, 100 DAYS IN A ZEN MONASTERY
1.17.92

Philip: smooth-skinned reassuring old man. Motherly. Cranky. Philip is an
OBJECT. Large, soft, bear-elephant w/clever speech. ". . .born difficult by
temperament: highly sensitive, poorly adaptable, negative in mood, or disor-
ganized." My feet have cracked like his.

david meltzer
FIRST AND LAST

First & last: the delight his work provides, & of course the lights. A day & nightbook blessed (& blessing) continuum of what's up in the noticing: what passes by the mind moving through its scales. His work is transparently devious & delirious & resists academic shrink-wrap, even though he's a scholar emeritus of the deepest reading & reflection. Like Whitman, Whalen likes to saunter through the world & the mind; unlike Walt, Whalen has a sense of humour & self-effacement. He resists monumentalizing via a sporadic & proactive relation to the 'seriousness' of poetry. He is a profound poet who giggles in the most profound moments.

Philip with Mr. Natural, circa 1985, Cerro Gordo Temple, Santa Fe
by permission of Suzi Winson

nancy victoria davis
FORK ENSO

Brit Pyland's house, San Francisco, 1988
photo by Rob Lee

jennifer birkett

Pink Dinosaurs Do Zen

Philip moved into Hartford Street Zen center when Issan got sick. That's when I first met him.

Friends dying too fast & too soon. Chamel house of AIDS epidemic. Temple. Hospice. Morphine comas & VNH nurses. Spiritual teachers & sudden joy. Men in sequin gowns totters on high heels, singing gospel & holding hands. "In the 70's we brought you disco, now we will teach you how to die." Then ashes on altar. *Om Tara.* Poof gone.

Sitting still in meditation hall. Facing the wall with lipstick on. Breath not steady. Closet new-age healer just here for the scene.

"Just sit" Philip would advise, "you have too many notions."

He was a gentleman if you treated him right. Got mad if you annoyed him and sang when happy.

Mostly he said, "You are a good girl," but one evening he paused at the entrance of the meditation hall & announced loudly, "Here comes the whore of Babylon." Carrying incense behind him to the altar, red as a beet & barely daring to breathe. Maybe he was talking about himself.

Every night before zazen, Philip sat in the living room dressed in black priest robes & held court. "Some guy from India is leading you down the garden path; he should be ashamed of himself." Or elaborate on the eye infection ruining his sight, "Woke up this morning and saw low grade pink dinosaurs everywhere like wallpaper in a cheap motel room – dinosaurs even on my underwear. I got a glimpse of what Blake said, "To see through the eye and not of it." Experience delusion and know you are deluded. Gradually, all the dinosaurs peeled away."

One time Myo asked, "What is the answer to it all?"

"Love," he replied. "At the bottom of the whole shebang is Buddha's passionate drive to end the suffering of stars, fish, people and everything."

Location Meditation

Philip said he would keep sitting zazen until he couldn't wriggle any longer. Then he got sick. Two years flat on his back, wearing hospital gowns & green wool hat.

Laguna Honda Hospice. Open ward. Clattering carts. Soft squish of nurse shoes. Medical bracelet with his name on it. Bed that goes up and down when you push different buttons. Food delivered on plastic tray. TV tuned to nature programs & fuzzy animals having sex or killing each other. Judge Judy. He enjoyed shock shows of American values gone cuckoo — scantly clad teenage girls with huge breasts screaming at their mothers.

Almost blind & sometimes he gets lost in sounds all around. Sudden fits where he's convinced he's in another building or place. "I'm not wearing any pants and my coattails are dragging in the mud." Hood River Oregon for lunch with Joanna McClure then back to San Francisco for a parade in the afternoon.

Knows he's unstuck in time — "It's like being on a movie set. The leading lady is late because she's waiting for her nail polish to dry. And the leading man is drunk or else fell off his chair and is lying on his back like a bug." This gets us into Kafka & cockroaches.

Then he wants something salty not sweet. Fritos hit the spot. Life lately reminds him of the soap opera with the hourglass & sand running through it. Days of Our Lives. We are always slipping away.

Bridge Between Worlds

Philip all bunched up in bed, upset, says he has lost his mind. "Local authorities insist I'm in California at a hospice."

Where are you really?

"Out in the country on a bridge. It's a very high bridge. There is a man singing on the bridge. I'd rather be in the previous town, Cherryville, on the road that leads to Mt. Hood. My parents had a cabin there by a creek."

Is it a bridge that kids like to jump off of?

"No, too dangerous. There are rocks and fire below. It is the bridge that throws things over. It's a very high bridge and things fall off. People and horses."

We hang out on the bridge for a long time.

Oxygen tank hissing a few beds down. Someone moans as nurse turns them over. Philip keeps getting distracted by an open sewer in the upper right field of his vision that has nasty breath. When a whiny voice complains they are tired of ice cream, Philip rolls his eyes and makes funny noises.

Then he hears a bell — "a single passionate bell" & knows where he is. "In the hospice," he says.

"Do you have a flashlight?" He wants to know when I leave.

I have a lighter.

"Good. Have a good night baby."

Dead & Full Empty

Sat with Philip today.

What's left of him. Brown Zen robes, icy cold, quite dead.

Wait politely until formal meditators leave before rushing over to his corpse to see if any Philip is left inside.

Tove feels some Phil over his heart.

Steve gazes at Philip then kisses him. "He looks pretty empty."

Full of empty.

Steve once asked Phil if he wanted a statue created of him after death.

"A glass jar with a mosquito in it."

Raspberry Cream-mate.

Woodlawn memorial Chapel. Philip in a cardboard box draped with red velvet.

After Socrates milkshake. Teacher in a box.

Baker-roshi glances at him pensively. "It is only Philip's body; the rest of him is in all of us.

We cast off our body like an old pair of pants."

Philip in another temporary container. Raspberries and flowers tossed inside I snitch a raspberry and gobble it down. "Bad girl," says Michael. "Smells good," says Amy.

Then into the furnace he goes. Metal room. Square trapdoor in back wall. Rushing sound of gas about to ignite the flames. Doors clang shut. Wave goodbye with faithful sigh.

Can hear him saying, "Be moved aside to who you are and what is really happening.

In the life of Zen practice you shouldn't come out alive."

Come back soon. I miss you.

19:7:02

sandor burstein
A LETTER

Dear Michael,

You suggested that I write a few recollections of Philip Whalen, the man, not the poet. Philip has been a friend to Beth and me for many years, and our hearts are filled with warmth whenever we think or speak of him.

It is difficult to try to remember when we first met. Perhaps it was in the old Beatnik days when Beth discovered life, poetry, and adventure in North Beach. Perhaps it was during one of the long-ago street fairs where I picked up broadsheets from local artists. No matter, we feel as if we'd known and admired Philip forever.

Beth is a flower-arranger trained in Japanese artistry over many years. When we were invited to witness Philip's ordination as a Zen priest, Beth had the pleasure and honor of making a floral offering for Philip's room. She still smiles happily when she recalls Philip's joy on that occasion.

Philip went to Japan to study. On our initial visit to that country, Philip learned that we were in his vicinity, and gave up several days to entertain and educate us. He showed us so much beauty, opening our eyes to gardens and temples that we have remained continuously in his debt. His influence pervades our lives.

When we all returned here, Philip came in and out of our lives in many ways. When he became ill, I was humbly honored to be his medical advisor. Beth sent Ikebana arrangements to his hospital rooms. When he improved, we loved to have him visit our home when he could. Philip knew of my love for books and brought me special copies of his poetic works when they came out. I treasure them, not just as books, but as loving gifts from a dear friend.

There is much more to say; there are more feelings to express. Suffice it for now for us to express our profound gratitude for being able to know, admire, and love this gentle man.

Sandor, and for Beth Burstein

photo by Neil Jacobs

joanna mcclure
A PHIL WHALEN SPECIALLY REQUESTED EVENING MEAL

7:30 pm – coffee with cream and sugar — medium strong, please.
apple pie — with ice cream if there is some.

9:00 pm – roqueford cheese and crackers from in the cupboard.
french olives — both kinds, please.
glass of Merlot 1999.

9:30 pm – hash browns with sausage and catsup.
.

. . . . . .

Critiques: pie has too much cinnamon.
not too much cheese on each cracker, please.
Merlot a bit sour but okay.
olives quite fine.
hash brown and sausage — better than those burnt meatballs.

Menu recorded at Zen Hospice by J. McClure sometime in 2001.

lawrence ferlinghetti

Philip Whalen, another great voice in the world of poetry, in these years that have already taken so many into silence, and Philip's still heard, one of the most distinctive, at once universal, urban, bucolic, cranky, and satiric—as if he were of another age—a Juvenal turned Buddhist. *Avé!*

2-17-01

Allen Ginsberg, Philip, Lawrence Ferlinghetti at City Lights Book Store, San Francisco, 1988
photo by Rob Lee

Philip and Bill Berkson blowing out candles, SF Art Institute
photo by Steven C. Wilson

Philip and Gregory Corso, 1993
photo by Christopher Felver

michael rothenberg
SEPTEMBER 17: AIRPORT TELEPHONE INTERZONE

"A lap of dead breakfast
and a telephone hidden under the blankets
They're moving me to the skilled nursing wing"

      Well, that's the right direction
      Better than the morgue

"I don't think at the morgue they fuss with you so
much, or so noisy"

      How do you feel?

"The same, tired (at other times 'lumpy')
They're keeping me 12 more days"

      At least I'll know where to find you
      when I get back

"I guess"

          *

      SFO airport to LA
      for celebratory reading
      at Beyond Baroque
The Diamond Noodle, p. 64:
u) World of Letters (editing & publishing,
criticism, journalism, all the public and
annoying side of writing)
v) Art World, ie. the mechanical, public side
of it: the gallery, theater, the concert hall & c

*

Mr. Whaaleen? Mr. Whaaleen?
Do you know where you are?

"Rome!"

"How can ya mess up macaroni & cheese?
And they put these big green peas next to it
to make it look scary"

Nancy brought you a burger
yesterday

"I don't remember"

Are you not remembering a lot?

"Yes"

Well, I won't let you forget
anything important

"I'm getting old and my memory is going"

Did you not remember
before you went in to the hospital?

"Yes"

*

MOTEL TELEPHONE INTERZONE

What shall I tell people
at the reading tomorrow?

"I've said"

That's what you want me to say?
`I've said'?

"Yes"

Cosmos Rothenberg, Michael Rothenberg, Philip, and Joanne Kyger at Joanne's,
April 12, 1992
photo by Nancy Victoria Davis

Philip with Cosmos Rothenberg
Hartford Street Zen Center, 1991
Photo by Rob Lee

Philip with Cosmos
Hartford Street, January 1, 2000
photo by Nancy Victoria Davis

Philip at Hartford Street Zen Center, 1997
photo by John Suiter

bill berkson
PHILIP WHALEN

Bagatelle [French from Italian *bagatella*] — 1. Trifle. 2. any of various games involving the rolling of balls into scoring areas — basket, hoop, net, goalpost, strike zone . . . Bingo! 3. A short literary or musical piece in light style.

Zip, zip, zip: I always think of the lines of Philip Whalen's poems as slicing clean across the page. Light, fast, irritable, alert to the "rollings" of those balls. I don't mean to suggest that Philip wrote trifles. Quite the contrary, the slightest Whalen has an urgency put behind each syllable, ample and articulate in the way of the big-band-music of classic poetry (in English, we call it "Elizabethan" for short).

Philip's fullness, *orotondo com' il circolo di Giotto,* round as Giotto's (freehand) circle.

Wanting to write, not knowing what or how, I toss through pages of Whalen. The random articulation gives one hope; his goofiness corrective of everybody else's self-importance.

Philip was like this in person, too. About eight years ago — 1994, I think — he gave a Dharma lecture at the Page Street Zen Center on Life and Death — that was his title, he could handle that. He prefaced the talk by saying, in that precise vibraphone treble phrasing of his: "I've got all kinds of things wrong with me, I could croak any time."

"Croak" forever after will ring up a Whalenesque timbre to my ear. Even so, I'd rather he hadn't.

August 30, 2002

tom clark
PHIL

The plum-lacquered woven Japanese basket Phil
    lately back from Kyoto gave us,
        Juliet's baby bed on Nymph & Cherry
The year Phil dwelt over on Larch with Don
Beyond the shimmering silver dollar eucalypti,
Sometimes strolled two dirt road blocks to visit,
People mad at him if he came over, if he didn't
    he later recollected.
Toting his laundry downtown, two sad sacks.
Later on camped down on Terrace tender
    dear heart crotchety and alone
In the same town with the vivacious Muse
Not quite on the outs & not quite on the ins w/ her,
        impatient
      amid nasturtiums
One day on acid sternly informed me, Thomas Clark,
Poetry will never get written this way.

charles bernstein
sorrow where there is no pain

what marks here? score skids, fill up

like the ice-tea truck my grandmother kept forgetting

before the wave closed over the gap

& none the wetter for it

or that gives you something to wail in

for Philip Whalen
(6.8.02)

jane falk
AN APPRECIATION OF PHILIP WHALEN'S
THE DIAMOND NOODLE

The first time I read *The Diamond Noodle,* I had just finished reading
Whalen's novels, *You Didn't Even Try* and *Imaginary Speeches for a Brazen
Head. Diamond Noodle* seemed puzzling and unconventional in compari-
son. A year later fresh from reading Whalen's early poetry collected in *Like
I Say* and *Memoirs of an Interglacial Age,* written about the same time that
Diamond Noodle was begun, my mind was zapped. I got it. What had once
seemed a cryptic and puzzling title made sense. Ostensibly about an impor-
tant year in its protagonist's life, the novel actually demonstrates an under-
standing of time and consciousness in Buddhist terms, presented through
the perspective of the diamond noodle, which readers learn can look "back-
wards and split your head 1000 ways."

As a collection of prose takes, *Diamond Noodle* moves back and
forth in time through various modes of consciousness at giddy pace. The
novel ends as the hero "gets" the first sentence of his unwritten book:
Wallace Bridge across the Yamhill River near where his parents grew up and
thus a bridge to his own beginnings. In terms of the novel's structure, the
allusion to Wallace Bridge also recalls the novel's opening prose take which
ends with the bridge's introduction. These are the kinds of intricate twists
Whalen creates in a novel which provides not vicarious experience but real
time participation in mental process.

Diamond Noodle's structure presents Whalen's superimposition of
the teachings of the Avatamasaka and Diamond Sutras on the understand-
ing of time expressed by the Buddhist concept of *pratitya-samutpada,* a
teaching understood to mean that all phenomena condition each other and
envisioned as a twelve-link chain of causation. The primary teaching of the
Avatamasaka Sutra, demonstrating the interdependence and interpenetra-
tion of all phenomena, is exemplified by the Net of Indra, a net of pearls

hanging over Indra's palace so that each pearl reflects all the others, similarly to the prismatic reflections of the diamond noodle. The Diamond Sutra teaches that all existence is empty of reality, consisting only of projections of the mind. The way the protagonist re-presents, remembers, and returns to the same experiences throughout the novel with subtle variations as one memory acts on and conditions another is part of its fascination, its upaya, and Whalen's power as a writer.

What Whalen's work gives us if we are receptive is the ability to inhabit our world with a new perspective. I write these lines while listening to the hum of the refrigerator, an ambulance siren, and thunder rumble. I am also in my mind on the page simultaneously writing, reading, and remembering the moment I understood the implications of Whalen's play with words. *Diamond Noodle* is food for thought.

Summer Solstice
2002

Philip, photo by Tom Pendergast

bruce holsapple
A DIRTY BIRD IN A SQUARE TIME: WHALEN'S POETRY

"Anatman" or nonself, a central tenet in Buddhist thought, derives from the insight that ego is transitory, that self is not an essence but an aggregate, something conditioned. An informal translation might be "the perception of emptiness of self." I think this insight into the emptiness of self provides a useful way to talk about Phil Whalen's poetry, although I should add that by "emptiness of self" I don't mean self-abnegation, and I don't mean that Whalen writes "about" emptiness. When I speak of the perception of emptiness in Whalen's poetry I mean a kind of detachment or self-regard—the Buddhist term is "mindfulness"—which I relate back to his remark (in the late fifties) that his poetry is "a picture or graph of a mind moving" (Overtime 50), since at the least that statement suggests height-ened self-scrutiny, mind watching mind. I see that self-scrutiny as a key fea-ture of Whalen's work. Again informally, Buddhists "practice" this insight into the emptiness of self, the effects of which transform daily life. Whalen was a practicing Buddhist,[1] so one expects that his practice has effected his verse. The effect is most readily seen in the content of the poems, but the detachment is also evident in certain techniques, like phrasing and voice, and can be seen in his methods of composition, where, for instance, the form that the poem takes becomes an explicit part of the poem's content. In the following, I'd like to show how Whalen's poems have been shaped by this insight into or detachment from self—in content, technique, and method—and how, consequently, what begins as self-exploration becomes a way to eclipse self.

Part of the story behind Whalen's poetry involves Kenneth Rexroth, for Whalen's early work owes much to the model Rexroth provided, espe-cially the historical context. That context includes an active Greek and Roman tradition in combination with a conspicuously Eastern disposition, albeit one shaped by a Modernist sensibility.[2] Rexroth passed that context on (as well as his use of landscape) to both Whalen and Snyder, and you can also see, in both, the early poetry used as a site for philosophical inter-rogation, just as with Rexroth. Whalen's "Sourdough Mountain Lookout" provides a good example, with its dedication to Rexroth, its use of landscape and its quotes from Heraclitus, Empedocles and Buddha. The poem was written in 1955-6 and proceeds (somewhat analogically) as a meditation on the transitory and on individual purpose or identity, a theme I'll pursue here. It's set in the North Cascades where Whalen was stationed as a fire lookout, makes conspicuous reference to immensities of earth and sky, and has an almost geologic context. In his discussion of time, landscape and identity, Whalen pulls together Western notions of multiplicity, flux and oneness with Buddhist concepts of the transitory and the Void in order to situate himself in that landscape both physically and metaphysically.

Within this philosophical context, Whalen employs a standard subject/object paradigm, formulated as Self and World, and he parallels that binary with several others, for instance, wakefulness and sleep, day and night, love and strife, but most importantly, the One and the Many, for he is concerned with reconciling the unity of experience with its polarities. Towards the conclusion of the poem, Whalen imagines the mountains surrounding his lookout cabin to be a "circle of 108 beads, originally seeds / of ficus religiosa / Bo-Tree" (Overtime 19). As readers probably know, the Buddha attained enlightenment meditating under a Bo-Tree. The beads exemplify diversity, the Many, but there's "one odd bead / Larger than the rest and bearing / A tassel (hair-tuft) (the man who sat / under the tree)..." The unity of the World, Whalen says, is provided by the emptiness at its center: "In the center of the circle, / A void, an empty figure containing / All that's multiplied; / Each bead a repetition, a world / Of ignorance and sleep" (19). As Buddha once sat, so now Whalen sits. What we see as phenomena is Void.

One other image deserves note, for Whalen also conceives of the universe as an egg, with Self emerging as a bird does, by transforming "molecules of albumen / To beak and eye / Gizzard and craw" (Overtime 18). Consequently, Self is understood as composed of the World to which it posed in opposition (as a binary); Self mirrors the World. Consider then how he writes about "mind" as he reaches the conclusion to "Sourdough Mountain Lookout"; that is, how mind is said to be both of the World and in the World:

> What we see of the world is the mind's
> Invention and the mind
> Though stained by it, becoming
> Rivers, sun, mule-dung, flies—
> Can shift instantly
> A dirty bird in a square time
> (Overtime 20)

Mind has invented the World it perceives, but it has invented this perceived World from the World it's composed of, the prior egg. That invention may stain the mind, but mind is inherently free of its inventions, "can shift instantly," like a bird in flight. This shifting about I also see as central to Whalen's poetry, and I'll speak of it again. I should mention though that "mind" is not Self and that this freedom of mind carries a further corollary, namely, a distrust of those products or inventions that stain the mind.

Whalen's equivocal conclusion to "Sourdough Mountain Lookout" allows for both the unity and multiplicity of the World, Void and phenomena, but that is largely because he won't acknowledge either as having priority, chicken and egg; he simply sets them in parallel. His conclusion is: "I'm still on the mountain" (Overtime 20). That equivocation emerges in another early poem "The Same Old Jazz" (1957), where he argues explicitly for duality, a distinction between subject and object, illusion and reality, rather than for the unity of both, as Buddhist doctrine states. The poem opens:

> OK, it's imperishable or a world as Will
> & Idea, a Hindu illusion that our habits continuously
> Create. Whatever I think, it
> Keeps changing from bright to dark, from clear
> To colored: Thus before I began to think and
> So after I've stopped, as if it were real & I
> Were its illusion
>
> But as Jaime de Angulo said, "What's wrong with two?"
> (On Bear's Head 14)

The opening lines concede that the illusion of World is "imperishable" and that this illusion—or invention—perpetuates the duality of experience, dark and bright.[3] This illusion is posited as prior to the subject experiencing it, so that any existent "Self" which emerges must be built from illusion, must be illusory. But this involves a paradox, doesn't it? For the perceiver must be real, in order for that illusion to occur, and if we grant the perceiver reality, doesn't that require that the World be real also? Why not simply accept the paradox, Whalen argues, that World is both reality and illusion?

The poem continues:

> So Sunday morning I'm in bed with Cleo
> She wants to sleep & I get up naked at the table
> Writing
> And it all snaps into focus
> The world inside my head & the cat outside the window

> A one-to-one relationship
> > While I imagine whatever I imagine
> > (On Bear's Head 14)

The relationship between the World "outside" (as object) and the representation of that World "inside" the speaker perhaps comes from Schopenhauer, as the opening lines imply, but the relationship is just as likely part of that subject/object paradigm mentioned above, a paradigm troubled by the very nature of thought, as Whalen himself soon understands. That is, the World and its representation in mind are not in "a one-to-one relationship," as he posits here. But Whalen's point again seems to be about the freedom of the mind from its illusions, "While I imagine whatever I imagine," because from here on the poem develops largely as a narrative about the transforming effects of love, about Cleo. Such effects would entail a clear sense of purpose and a distinction between illusion and reality. Notice then that the poem concludes with the same equivocation seen in "Sourdough Mountain Lookout":

> She'll go away. I'll go away. The world will go away.
> ("The idea of emptiness engenders compassion
> Compassion does away with the distinction
> between Self & Other . . .")
> But through her everything else is real to me & I have
> No other self.
> "What's wrong with two?"
> > (On Bear's Head 16)

To restate the closing lines in terms of that subject/object paradigm: There's no other Self than that Self which the World provides, so even granting this World as illusory or empty, the World is nevertheless what makes us "real"; and in this case, sexual love provides a basis for individual purpose and identity.[4] But what's wrong with two, to answer Whalen's question, is that the phenomenon of Self emerges from the Void, as does the World, and these "two" are both illusory; the Void is neither one nor two; hence, the pleasures of sexual love are also illusory; and Whalen is too circumspect to stay satisfied with that kind of answer. One can trace his explorations beyond it in several other early poems, such as in "All About Art & Life," written two years later (composed "28:viii:59—9:ix:59").

It's important to mark first, though, that the reality or illusion of World (and Self) is an important early concern of Whalen's, and that these poems show him working from a Modernist dichotomy between subject and object, with the World identified as the object of knowledge and Self identified as the individual agent or experiencer. To anticipate, what Whalen moves towards is an understanding of Self and World as fundamentally the same, without division, and both as empty. In "All About Art & Life," for example, Whalen starts to argue against evaluations of good and bad, love and hate, as modes of identity or self-knowledge, because such judgments are so obviously relative: "Why bother to say I detest liver / & adore magnolia flowers / Liver keeps its flavor the blossoms / drop off / & reappear, whoever / cares, counts, contends" (On Bear's Head 91). As he remarks a few lines later, to make such judgments is "merely talking to hear my head rattle." But there is a different way of perceiving the World, and in that poem Whalen tries to refocus: "Not I love or hate: // WHAT IS IT I'M SEEING // & // WHO'S LOOKING" (On Bear's Head 91). Here Whalen steps back from acts of ascription in order to look at ascription itself, steps back to look at identity, and the poem functions as a mode of self-interrogation, a way to explore Self and World. What he implicitly argues for (evident in the capitalization) is a more direct way of perceiving the World, one not based on superficial states of identification, same and different, or further, not based on the duality of Self and World, the very concept that he argued for in "The Same Old Jazz."[5] This resolution can be amplified with a poem written earlier that same year, "I Return To San Francisco" (written "20:iii:59—15: iv:59"). For instance, Whalen writes there:

> While I'm looking for sleep
> Bright shapes of day bedevil my eyes
> identification with one's "good" qualities
> and vice versa—where does that put you?
> identification with neither—what do you call that?
> or with both?
> With ANYTHING ELSE . . . shape, form, quality, mode
> > what then?
> "What was your original face, before you were conceived?"
> (On Bear's Head 86)

As I said above, identification is singled out in these poems because it is so obviously relative, but there is a deeper problem here, namely that Whalen is acutely aware that the mind is disposed to such attributions (positive and negative) and that the mind shapes the experience it supposedly receives from the World. For instance, (again) in "All About Art & Life," Whalen writes: "It comes to us straight & flat / My cookie-cutter head makes shapes of it // CHONK: 'scary!' / CHONK: 'lovely!' / CHONK: 'ouch!'" (On Bear's Head 91). The disposition to ascribe positive or negative values—the Buddhist terms would be attachment and aversion—distorts as it receives experience. How would you respond, Whalen asks, if you didn't sort by yes and no, good and evil, and as his quote on "original face" indicates, the question invokes a famous Zen koan from Hui Neng's Platform Sutra. One's response to that koan reveals one's penetration into the fundamental unity of Self and World, illusion and reality. There is no division between who you are and what you perceive.

Collectively, then, the above four poems provide some sense of the way Whalen understood the problem of "Self" or identity in the 1950s, namely as suspect, perhaps a construction, but the poems also provide an important context to his well-known remark that his "poetry is a picture or graph of a mind moving, which is a world body being here and now which is history . . . and you" (Overtime 50). The remark was made at the end of Memoirs of an Interglacial Age—entitled "Since You Ask Me (A Press Release, October 1959)"—and written within months of "All About Art & Life" and "I Return To San Francisco." So at the very least, Whalen's stated problems with illusion and self-identity play an important role in the notion of "graphing" the mind.[6] Moreover, such statements show that in 1959 Whalen was methodically taking "Self" as his object, with the plausible corollary that mind was understood as not only in process but as a process, and—to use a term from "Sourdough Mountain Lookout"—a process constantly in the act of invention. That said, the pivotal term in Whalen's formulation (above) is the verb "moving," since it's the activity of mind, rather than its content, which has priority, i.e. recognizing mind in its acts of construction. And I think this is the more important point, for it is in acts of construction that Whalen's detachment is most clearly seen. Bear in mind also that this movement of mind relates back to the capacity of mind to shift instantly as in "Sourdough Mountain Lookout," because of its inherent freedom from its inventions, and finally, that configurations of Self are likely such inventions. Here's why I find that crucial: The consequence of this freedom from Self is a poetry grounded neither in representations of Self nor in objective statements about the World—the polarities—but rather grounded between those two in the activities or motions of the mind (understood to be a world body).

One other point needs development, namely, that Whalen's stated concerns with perception and identity and his goal of documenting the movement of mind as a "world body" involve a kind of splitting or detachment. Whalen's purpose in the 1950s was no doubt to see into or develop insights about his own self-nature, if only to transcend routine ways of perception, such as his conditioned likes and dislikes. But in order to look into or listen to that Self in its construction, a suspension from Self occurs. That suspension or detachment stands in contrast to normative processes of cognitive investment, processes in the construction of self-identity. Further, this suspension from Self is a key element in allowing a different kind of poetry to emerge, for what begins as self-exploration soon becomes a way to go beyond limitations of Self. As a consequence, the poem is no longer understood as a mode of self-expression, and what the poem emerges from is not simply the poet's intent.[7] The poet's intention plays an obvious role, but there is, in Whalen's work, a disposition to step back and listen to both Self and World.[8] This disposition entails a propensity to listen for something unexpected—to some extent inducing novelty in the poem—but it also involves a disposition to transcend expectation, transcend the limitations of Self, e.g. those normative, largely regulatory thought processes which compose the way we do things. Said a different way, whatever Self is, Self is always under construction. But mind is not Self, and the mind's constructive processes are potentially revelatory.

One place where a noticeable suspension from Self occurs is in those poems where Whalen addresses himself as speaker, for the speaker's role becomes conspicuously self-reflexive, dual. That is, Whalen's "I" becomes other. Whalen makes an important comment on that "I" in "Minor Moralia" (written mostly in 1959), where he writes, "I change, I tell myself, 'I' IS ONLY THESE PASSING STATES, THEIR ACTUAL PASSAGE" (sic; On Bear's Head 190). As his use of "only" and the capitalization indicate, this insight into the transitory nature of self-identity comes as something of a surprise. And we can tease out an important critical distinction about the dual role of "I" from this quote, for note that Whalen is discussing an experience of Self and that there is an implicit gap or distance between Self as an object of experience and Self as experiencer. That is because the "experienced Self" is composed of representations, is representational. This is in contrast to the agent "I" or speaking Self and the experiencing "I." In this quote, then, that experienced or represented Self is no longer adhered to, but rather seen as transitory, part of the world, marking the passage through various states of experience, as the reflection of one's agency. To repeat: this experience of Self is what is disengaged from.

Disengagement from our self-representations is a common enough event, but in Whalen's hands, the gap or displacement between "selves" allows for the evolution of a speaker who observes himself as "I" speaking, a doubling effect or "dialogic splitting" (I becomes you) which is standard in his work by the 1960s. He both occupies and does not occupy the lyric subject position. While he readily identifies himself as speaker, he just as readily steps aside, and that representation of Self never constitutes more than, as he says above, a kind of "passage." As a passage, however, it can be understood as an element of the mind in motion, and I would hazard that Whalen continually displaces that represented Self in his work by mediating between Self as agent and Self as experiencer, setting up rhetorical distance between the two, conspicuous in his use of pronouns. Importantly, from these early notions of Self and from this heightened self-scrutiny—taking that experienced Self as an object or other—there emerges one of Whalen's most striking poetic achievements, his renditions of fallibility. As an example, consider the final stanza of "What Are You Studying, These Days?" The "you" and "I" are both Whalen:

> Your trouble is you're not very real, are you.
> Hallucinatory fountain pens, eh?
> Skin chips and flaky on the outside
> Internal organs all blackened and shriveled
> What do you expect with too much on mind
> Too busy to see or hear a single particular?
> I have put on a gown of power I didn't know I had—
> Or wanted.
>   (Overtime 293)

This mode of self-interrogation and these renditions of fallibility, often undermining the speaker's "authority," are commonplace in Whalen's poetry and probably overlooked because they're characteristic, part of his vast sense of humor. But this banter or self-talk is also a serious form of self-reflection, a very sophisticated kind of play. While such forms of self-address may have begun with early experiments—with "graphing" the mind[9]—as they develop in sophistication, they become a mode of self-disclosure and allow for something larger than "person" to emerge; they allow for the transpersonal to emerge, an eclipse of ego.

But to reiterate my main point, these acts of self-scrutiny that Whalen takes as his subject matter in the 1960s require a suspension or sense of detachment. The second phase of my argument is that this detachment or distance effects various aspects of the work, such as phrasing and voice, and finally that the detachment becomes procedural, a way of generating texts. Notice then below how "The Dharma Youth League" proceeds as a series of self-corrections, caused by that same kind of self-interrogation, and how the procedure effects both the poem's phrasing and pace. Take note also of Whalen's punctuation.

> I went to visit several thousand gold buddhas
> They sat there all through the war,—
> They didn't appear just now because I happen to be in town
> Sat there six hundred years. Failures.
> Does Buddha fail. Do I.
> Some day I guess I'll never learn.
> (Overtime 172)

This poem was written in 1966, probably in Japan, and initiated by visiting gold buddhas who "sat" (or meditated) throughout World War II. But as Whalen marvels, he qualifies himself because of several unstated conflicts. These conflicts operate as part of the subtext. For example, his comment that "They didn't appear just now because I happen to be in town" pre-supposes a prior thought, an initiating egocentricity, which this statement corrects. The supposed profundity of the gold buddhas' ability to sit, as another instance, is emblematic of a persistence Whalen wishes he had, so he then amplifies his statement about their sitting "all through the war" to "Sat there six hundred years." And a curious thought emerges there, as further evidence of conflict, for he then labels the buddhas "failures." Whalen does so perhaps because meditating buddhas don't actually "do" anything; they didn't stop the war. He doesn't explain why. But he's establishing a point, and at this point it's apparent that the poem partakes of a pendulum motion, back and forth. Whereas at first Whalen marvels, now he swings in the opposite direction and criticizes the buddhas, clearly a projection, for the new statement is also in error, and Whalen then moves to yet another position. By foregrounding this motion of mind over the propositional content, this motion becomes a dynamic part of the content, in fact, transforms the content, since the propositions are now suspended from a direct referential function. To an extent, the poet follows the mind's motion back and forth rather than identifies with any point of reference, for there's no overt position stated, and Whalen hasn't erased his acknowledged errors; they still operate as part of the text. Internal conflict, then, is the modus operandi from which a deeper perspective emerges, and Whalen apparently listens for and incorporates these conflicts, rather than suppresses them. But Whalen obviously doesn't believe these buddhas have failed, either, so there is a position established, albeit one which incorporates the conflict. This inclusiveness is part of a method, and it's made possible by detachment; a detachment in explicit contrast to arguing for a proposition about gold buddhas or the mind.

Another point: The poem proceeds one phrase at a time, is composed of "phrasings," rather than larger conceptual units (such as clauses in an argument). Composing from the phrase allows Whalen to shift direction or improvise with each new phrase, but any shift also involves listening closely to himself and a kind of flexibility, for this entails "following" the poem.[10] That is, the poem's oscillation, back and forth, occurs as a consequence of stepping back and listening to Self, even as he engages Self. Consequently, "The Dharma Youth League" extends as a series of oscillating phrases or corrections, each building on its predecessor, until the poem finally turns back to the source of error, arrives at the doorstep of Self, with "Do I." That question discloses the poem, to some extent, as a meditation on the efficacy of Whalen's own meditation practice. The Buddha obviously doesn't fail, and according to Buddhist belief, Whalen and the Buddha are one, so by extension he doesn't fail either. His twisted last line ("Some day I guess I'll never learn") has to do with achieving "Original Mind" through meditation, getting beyond self-conflict, for Whalen's resolve is that he must drop such corrective thought processes "some day." Paradoxically, when that happens, he'll find himself right where he always has been—since all mind is Original Mind—already beyond those thought processes. This then is the same freedom of mind posited in "Sourdough Mountain Lookout," freedom from the products of mind, from thought itself, the inventions. The poem works by taking these thought processes as both its content and its procedure, explicitly takes thought as its subject and it's mode of pursuit, and Whalen's focus is as much on these processes—the motion of the mind—as it is on content. Moreover, the progression of thoughts is composed of inward turns. As Whalen twists inward, the phrases shorten. These inward turns or moments of self-recognition in fact generate the text and provide an example of how Whalen's detachment shapes the phrasing of the poem, since the turns are made possible by a cultivated inner space, by watchfulness.

Note also that Whalen's interrogatives lack question marks. The lack of punctuation or the use of periods instead of question marks signals of course that he has no intention of answering those questions—they're statements, rhetorical questions, one a marker of self-reflection ("Do I"). The overall effect is that as statements the interrogatives chart the progression of Whalen's thoughts, "mind moving," in a kind of short hand. But the lack of question marks and the innovative punctuation are also part of the rhetorical dimension of Whalen's work, related to use of voice, in this case intonation. That use of voice emerges from the same kind of detachment.[11] Consider, for example, the way he manipulates voice in the following "Homage to WBY."

> after you read all them books
> all that history and philosophy and things
> what do you know that you didn't know before?
> Thin sheets of gold with bright enameling
> (On Bear's Head 112)

Whalen's use of direct address can be misleading, but perhaps it's obvious here that the lack of capitalization and punctuation, misuse of "them" and the poorly paralleled direct objects in the first two lines convey a speaker being belligerently dumb, and that this is in contrast with Yeats's supposed learning. If you imagine this poem as involving only that one voice and imagine that belligerent speaker as representing Whalen, you probably miss the point. The belligerent voice in effect "compliments" Yeats, for that voice is not only deliberately dumb, it's undermined by the shift in tone at the end. The third line mediates between the two "voices" and poses a legitimate question. The compliment isn't without ambiguity. But Whalen also was a scholar, as scholarly as Yeats was, and Whalen's "homage" consists of the transition to that final line, with the positive image of enameled gold, the skilled use of vowels, the capitalized "Thin" and rimed "enameling." These are in contrast to the undistinguished "things" in line two, the miming in the first two lines juxtaposed to the concluding trope. This use of voice is central to the construction of the poem and, as said, emerges from the same detachment from Self.

Use of voice contributes to the emotional complexity of Whalen's poetry, and I'd like to talk of that emotional complexity briefly, but the point requires qualification, because (again) I don't mean that Whalen is writing "about" an emotion, nor is he simply motivated by an emotion, and I don't mean to imply that emotional complexes and images are fully distinguishable from ideas. It's apparent however that emotional complexes and images are not used simply to reinforce themes in Whalen's poems; they aren't subordinate to ideas, and in Whalen's poetry they often are used as registers significant in and of themselves, with the same force that a proposition has. In the simplest terms, what's of chief concern is the feeling produced by a poem, not the ideas elaborated on, for what motivates the poetry is largely experiential, sometimes a matter of sensibility. This focus on feeling and sensibility is related back to the notion of graphing the mind, as distinguished from developing "statements" about the World, as well as to the dynamic organization of the poem. To an extent, the same could be said for many poems, i.e. that they are importantly experiential rather than ideological. But in Whalen's case the watchfulness or detachment balances with the assertion, listening with speaking, such that his detachment alters his phrasing. The main impulse is centrifugal, expansive, yet in Whalen's phrasing there is often a strange inward curve or reflexivity, evident, for example, in his renditions of fallibility.

One place to look at Whalen's detachment in tandem with the emotional underpinning of the poem is in "Weather Odes," composed in 1972, though for brevity I'll concentrate on the first two (of six) sections. Here is the opening:

> Just before I fell asleep
> In the middle of the afternoon
> I told myself, "It is NOW
> That I must work that change make
> That move which will be the foundation
> For that spectacular success which must illumine
> All my later days"
> (Heavy Breathing 114)

This section is framed by its reportorial opening clause and is obviously self-reflexive, so one can produce thematic readings. But surely the point is the funny dichotomy between what the speaker says he'll do and what he's about to do, i.e. fall asleep after making an inflated resolution to change. That is to say, the experience of reading this section is importantly emotional, and we are provided with that emotional experience—we feel it—several ways. There is, obviously, the sense of humor, for terms like "foundation," "spectacular," and "must illuminate" are conspicuously inflated terms, formal in register. The phrasal extensions—the chaining effect caused by varied uses of "that" and "which"—produce another kind of inflation, as do the rhythms, for the rhythms push forward, noticeable in the percussive use of /m/, "must," "make," "move" "my." So this isn't simply reportage, even though it presents itself that way, and it's of critical importance to note that Whalen has constructed rather than simply captured the dichotomy between what he says and what he does. That is, the insights and emotions involved, perplexity, irony, false resolve and sense of self-absorption, are produced by the poem. They are moreover shaped by the two subject positions established, the speaker who observes and reports to us, and the speaker who is the object of observation, the one who had originally addressed himself, making the resolution to change. The two speakers are of course identical, but notice that the first selectively reports on the second—himself—as a somewhat unregenerate "other," that this reporting Self is noticeably smarter, and that he has an insight that the other lacks. Notice also that the distinguishing insight emerges from experiencing Self as a representation—in common parlance, by listening to oneself speak, in distinction to "engaging" Self—and that this insight is the very antithesis of self-absorption. In fact, the speaker's detachment here indicates that he is not at all self-absorbed, and part of the emotion generated by the poem arises from a kind of torsion between the two positions, self-absorbed and self-aware. In terms of my argument, the emotions generated by this section arise from that central insight into Self, an insight that shapes the phrasing (e.g. the use of rhythm). But that is also to say that emotions and phrasing are both the result of a detachment from Self and further are the result of a literary practice. In effect, the actual author situates himself between two positions, Self speaking and Self listening, agent and experiencer, assertion and reception, just as he does in "The Dharma Youth League," an oscillation which the poem "graphs."

This opening passage is terminated with three asterisks and followed by the second section. The link between the two is perhaps one of topical or chronological extension, but it is also importantly emotional (recall Whalen's resolution to change):

> With a head full of sunlight
> What's killing you now?
>
> No patience to sit and watch the ivy grow
> No patience with sleep
>
> Exhausted by a band of mare's tails
> Moving down from the north
> Right across the sky from west to east
> (West is the beginning of Ocean)
> (Heavy Breathing 114)

The distinction made earlier between stating emotions and producing emotions can be demonstrated here, for although Whalen states emotions (e.g. no patience), the more important fact is, I think, that the piece produces emotions. One key emotion produced is that of exasperation—exasperation with Self. Again, rhetoric plays a role in this, with the use of hyperbole, for Whalen's three complaints about his malady all function to induce exasperation through a sense of conflict and entrapment, largely because of the underlying expectations.[12] One such expectation is that, when your head is full of sunlight (good weather), you should feel content. His lack of contentment relates back to the earlier uneasiness and resolution to change. But it obviously doesn't follow that, once content, one would then have the patience "to sit and watch the ivy grow," and it's part of the complexity of the poem that Whalen hasn't produced a convincing demand of himself in response to his cranky question about what's upsetting him. To expect such prolonged patience of himself—even humorously—is indicative of something more serious motivating the question. Again two subject positions emerge. One can tease out why the speaker wants change, for example, a sense of failure or stasis. But the point remains that the demands he makes of himself are motivated by a sense of exasperation and, further, the tensions produced in this section are actually felt by the reader as conflict rather than simply reported as such, even though Whalen reports his feelings. One could say, then, that the emotional dynamic, feeling, takes priority over the propositional content, the ideas, for that emotional dynamic is more properly the focus. That dynamic emerges because of a priority put on feeling, but it is also part of a method or procedure.

What's additionally important about emotion in a poem like "Weather Odes" is that the poem proceeds from section to section by unfolding that emotional dynamic. Here's why I think that's important. When Leslie Scalapino interviewed Whalen in the late 1980s, she apparently asked him whether one of his modes of composition was collage (Scalapino 1990, 108). Whalen explicitly said no, that his poems were not collage, a point that Scalapino reiterates in a second essay (1999, xvii). This is significant because Whalen's most obvious way of composing poems is by juxtaposition, placing passage beside disparate passage, just as in collage (and that's probably why Scalapino asked the question). Yet Whalen insisted the poems were an "interweaving of different strands of ideas or notes, sounds that come around and about and all make a strange harmony. Somehow the overall object has its own proportions and its own working parts inside but it's hard to see 'em I think" (Scalapino 1989, 109). That is to say, the poem is not simply pieced together, nor arranged as collage; there's an underlying connection. My point is fairly simple. The unity Whalen speaks of is often achieved by emotional linkages, sometimes by an emotional under-paneling between parts and, further, the complexity of the poems often consists of emotional juxtapositions whose linkage is felt rather than ideological. This is important because the progression of Whalen's poems is not simply propositional and not always thematic. Whalen's poems move in several ways, in several directions, but often on the basis of feeling, and feeling has its own rationales, its own dimension. As suggested, this involves a method or procedure that not only alters the content of the poem but also the dynamic, the way the poem moves.

I'd like to conclude by discussing another late poem, "Tassajara" (1972), in terms of its dynamic, or rather how detachment transforms Whalen's poetry from concerns with Self and identity to concerns with thought and nonthought, in effect eclipsing Self. For just as the self-interrogation evolves into a self-reflexive "banter" (and the renditions of fallibility) through a kind of dialogic splitting, so that same splitting effect or detachment further develops into an interrogation of one's thought processes, superseding considerations of Self. I also choose "Tassajara" because receptive processes here play an important role in resolving the subject/object dichotomy we began with; Whalen now provides us with a different model of that relationship; subject and object, Self and World, are understood as unified. But finally, with this poem, I'd like to show how the movement or progression of the poem—a movement that relates back to graphing the mind moving—has become an explicit part of the content, how the form becomes dynamic.

"Tassajara" is Tassajara Springs, the site of Zanshinji, the Zen Mountain Center (in California) where Whalen practiced as head monk in the late 70s. At one level, the poem is most obviously about his meditation practice, sitting in silence, as the first four lines indicate, and the poem enacts a moment of insight, kensho, although in this instance Whalen is probably having fun with us. The poem reads:

> What I hear is not only water but stones
> No, no, it is only compressed air flapping my eardrums
> My brains gushing brown between green rocks all
> That I hear is me and silence
> The air transparent golden light (by Vermeer of Delft)
> Sun shines on the mountain peak which pokes
> The sun also ablaze &c.
> Willard Gibbs, Hans Bethe, what's the answer
> A lost mass (Paris gone)
> Shine red in young swallow's mouth
> Takagamine Road

The water suffers
Broken on rocks worn down by water
Wreck of THE DIVINE MIND on the reef called Norman's Woe
"Suddenly, ignorance," the Shastra says.
Moon arises in my big round head
Shines out of my small blue eyes
Tony Patchell hollers "Get it! Get it!"
All my treasure buried under Goodwin Sands
(Overtime 247)

The poem unfolds in a series of associations and assertions, but the overall mode is one of self-observation. It begins with an analysis of sensation, and, as with "The Dharma Youth League," initially proceeds by inward turns; the initial misdirections are elements of a pattern, and they operate as both content and procedure. Mark also that the speaker practices an insight: the World is not "outside," but rather is indistinguishable from the speaker (e.g. "My brains gushing brown"). This initial recognition—or invocation—of nonduality, Self as World, induces a meditative silence. Here's the narrative thread. As the speaker settles into place, sunlight becomes noticeable and triggers a comparison to Vermeer (riming with hear), then an explicit observation of sunlight on the mountain. Other thoughts emerge. The sun is recognized as "ablaze" and that apparently invokes "energy," for we literally veer into a discussion of energy and mass. The two figures mentioned, Gibbs and Bethe, are theoretical physicists, Bethe concerned with solar energy. Ideas cluster here, as they often do in meditation. We shift from Gibbs and Bethe—presumably their attempts to solve the riddles of energy and matter—down through several fragmentary images to end with the phrase "Takagamine Road," a road in Kyoto leading to Takagamine Mountain. (Whalen lived in Kyoto for three years.) The two mountains are paralleled, one inside, one outside. But while "lost mass" follows from Gibbs and Bethe (mass and energy), the parenthetical "Paris gone" and image of the swallow are difficult to decode, perhaps intentionally so. Nevertheless they do function in emotive and associative ways; the mass is "lost" and Paris is "gone"—both figuratively consumed?—in contrast to positive integers like "shine," "red," "young," and the open swallow's mouth. Perhaps the point is we're drifting, in a moment of self-absorption. Perhaps the point is regeneration.

The stanza break after "Takagamine Road" is a procedural one, for the speaker stops reflecting and refocuses on the stream, shifts back to his point of concentration. And while the first stanza is largely descriptive, bounces from thought to thought, the second stanza is plotted. Water is said to "suffer" rocks, invoking Buddha's first noble truth, that all existence is characterized by suffering. The rocks likewise suffer water. Once the mind becomes clarified by this truth, thinking becomes "right thought," part of the Eightfold Noble Path. The passage also invokes the Buddhist concept of pratitya-samutpada or "interdependent origination," that all things arise interdependently. This moment of clarity then (perhaps about the interdependence of phenomena and suffering) is what shipwrecks THE DIVINE MIND—the gist being that the transcendent subject or Self is also interdependent and goes down with the ship. Self is not an essence but an aggregate, a transitory phenomenon. THE DIVINE MIND breaking against Norman's Woe parallels water breaking against rocks. But a second incident also occurs here, for Whalen appropriates from Olson's Maximus Poems. "Norman's Woe" is a reef in Gloucester and appears in "All My Life I've Heard About Many"; "divine mind" is cribbed from Melville's "Divine Inert" (Olson 177; Butterick 247-50). Olson's poem was composed in 1959, the year Whalen visited Olson in Gloucester, so the citation may have historical reference. I think moreover entrance of THE DIVINE MIND marks the point where a sly sense of humor becomes conspicuous; the tone shifts slightly; the gesture is histrionic. But notice that we don't lose focus, like before. There follows a citation from the Shastra, a classic Buddhist text, on our fundamental ignorance (emptiness), and with that citation the moon, a symbol of enlightened mind, rises inside the speaker, that is, after the shipwreck of DIVINE MIND. Inside and outside then are now identical, and the moonrise contrasts with the sunset (in the first stanza). While I don't know who Tony Patchell is, he functions somewhat like a Zen master, shouting "Get it! Get it!," a reference to the Ungraspable perhaps, a famous Zen paradox (get it?). So kensho, insight into the fundamental identity of Self and World (as Ungraspable), is invoked. Whalen's final line about Goodwin Sands makes reference to a breakwater off Kent on the coast of England, the site of frequent shipwrecks. This site is where he says that his "treasure" is now buried. Whalen's recognition of loss acts as the resolve, though perhaps "mimics a resolve" would be the more accurate phrase.

Several questions emerge from this reading which I have only provisional answers for, but it's obvious first off that the poem is initiated by listening to Self and that, secondly, it proceeds by following sequences of thought. The sequence of thoughts is given as the motion of the mind, but these thoughts emerge because the speaker is detached from that motion. A third point follows, in that the activity or motion of the mind is prioritized in the poem over content, for the poem's propositions are collectively far less important than its transitions, the movement between thoughts, progressions sometimes logical, sometimes not. Said a different way, the dynamic form—the motion of the poem—is an explicit part of the content, and perhaps could be said to eclipse propositional content as the poem's focal concern, in as much as it transforms that content. Again, it's Whalen's detachment from the subject position that makes that new focus possible. My fourth point would be a rejoinder that these thoughts don't proceed willy-nilly. "Tassajara" proceeds by establishing thought as its subject—to an extent by following thoughts—within a larger context that guides and eventually determines thought. That larger context is the practice of meditation, even though it's not likely that Whalen was actually meditating when he wrote this. The intention is to disengage from thought, and that intention plays an explicit role in the poem's content.

One problem remains. While following thoughts remains at the basis of this poem, as I said, the second stanza is more structured, more overtly informed by ideology, and perhaps also informed by an underlying stillness, the cessation of thought. In those terms, the line "'Suddenly, ignorance,' the Shastra says," becomes pivotal. That line seems to coincide with the sun setting, and from this posited darkness or ignorance, the moon emerges, importantly inside the speaker, rather than outside, which signals that Self has been eclipsed and that the speaker has arrived at the unity between inside and out, Self and World. This nonduality is obviously the poem's theme. I recognize that the juxtaposition of Patchell yelling "Get it!" with the final comment on buried treasure suggests loss, further, suggests searching for that treasure, but these lines are noticeably ambiguous, and tone here provides as much guidance as reference does. As I mentioned, a sly sense of humor enters at the wreck of THE DIVINE MIND, and something other may be at play. For Whalen's final line on Goodwin Sands implies distance and is subdued. A plausible reading might be, "All that I took as treasure is now buried under sand," with sand having an association with the transitory, time. But this is something of a storybook ending, isn't it? One senses an underlying joke, hence my comment that the resolve is mimicked. While this second stanza talks about loss and shipwreck, the comic effect of Patchell yelling "Get it!," Whalen's invocation of the Ungraspable, and the fictional treasure buried under "Goodwin Sands" (along with commonplace associations between ignorance, darkness and poverty), all work against taking that sense of loss too seriously. There's nothing lost if the World is an illusion, one might say, since there was actually nothing to have. Alternately, if Self is identical with the World, as the moon rising inside the

146   bruce holsapple

speaker seems to imply, there is nothing to lose, either.[13] So Whalen's con-
clusion might (so to speak) be taken with a grain of sand.

When Whalen was ordained Abbot of the Hartford Street Zen
Center in 1991, he said on officially assuming his position, "The seat is
empty. There is no one sitting in it. Please take good care of yourselves"
(Schelling and Waldman 224). The statement involves characteristic ironies,
if only because the seat will always remain empty; as he said in "Sourdough
Mountain Lookout," the center is void. Further, if no 'Self' occupies that
seat, responsibility shifts to the individual; "please take good care," or as
the Buddha advised, work out your salvation diligently. Those ironies aside,
however, this is clearly a statement of anatman, insight into non-self, and,
as I've tried to show, this insight is central not only to Whalen's medita-
tion practice, it's had a shaping effect on his verse. That shaping occurs on
several levels, most obviously in content, but also at the level of phrasing
and voice, and importantly it alters the dynamic form of the poems. I think
it has other consequences as well. His notion of "graphing" the mind, for
instance, in contrast to a poetic construed as making statements "about"
the World, led Whalen to a poetry less reliant on thematic development
and topical unity, less philosophical, more direct and inclusive, more quick
and wide ranging, a poetry based on the mind in motion, on immediate
perceptions and on emotion. Because principles of poetic unity consequently
change, the poems develop in a wild variety of ways. One aspect of this
"redirection" is Whalen's new ability to shift about, unconstrained by per-
spective, tone or logical bridgework. As I've also tried to show, that empha-
sis on the mind in motion transforms the poem, in as much as the motion
itself soon becomes a part of his message. That is, rather than securing a
philosophical perspective, establishing a stance, Whalen continually shifts
stance and perspective, disrupts thought, and undermines a fixed sense
of Self. These are procedures that inform the content, as they shape and
transform the content. Further, what begins as a mode of self-exploration
in Whalen's work now becomes a way to eclipse Self. The consequence is
a poetry grounded in the activity of mind, rather than poses or positions,
whether a theoretical stance, point of reference, or sense of identity. This
is brought about, I've argued, by a detachment from Self and that detach-
ment in turn results in a poetry which comes to take thought processes as
its object, rather than assertions of identity or value. That is as much to say
Whalen has found a way beyond Self by disengaging from constructions of
Self, letting Self drop away, as Dogen has it.

The consequence is a poetry of sometimes bizarre, but always
diverse emotional effects, constantly humorous and self-reflective, of enor-

mous but troubling appetites, of startling particularity, with wild variations in tone and with striking uses of vernacular. Whalen is, as Scalapino said, the most formally innovative of the Beats (1999, xv), and the poems unfold in a dazzling number of ways, in multiple directions, for mind and line can shift instantly, "a dirty bird in a square time." A poem starts, for example, from something as innocuous as the imperative to "Find twenty beautiful pages for Thomas Clark," but then begins by listing precious objects, "things hitherto unincluded," as in "October First":

> 5. Indian shrine, gift of J. Kyger
> 6. Blue Mexican glass pitcher
> 7. Three onyx eggs"
>   (Overtime 238)

That twenty item "treasury" accomplished, Whalen moves in a lateral direction by listing bizarre replacements for each one:

> 5-a. Curious dream of thunder and lightning
> 6-a. I am drinking buttermilk while I write this
> 7-a. WHUMP!

This twist sideways invokes a complication, namely, how one maintains value (the possession of treasures) in a world bent on change. But his obsession with replacements discloses a further insight, for as Whalen constructs his second list, he calls into question not only the value of those original objects, but the notion of value itself, and many of the new items conspicuously divert or captivate his attention in some way. What's at first considered precious, a valuable object, is now understood to fixate the attention, and, as we compulsively complete that second twenty item list, an "African daisy mantra" emerges, with the refrain, "UNGUM UNGUM UNGUM," which in turn morphs into several resolutions, e.g. "If the door knocks or the telephone rings / It's not my problem" (Overtime 236-8). But then mind can shift again, as Whalen has always said, and take us beyond whatever we've gummed ourselves to—those inventions staining the mind—and his conclusion (note the relationship of Self and World) reads like this:

> Outside as if suddenly happily naked
> Top of my head painlessly removed
> Effortless: beyond glad or tears in space beyond security
> outside

HUM !
The world really being I there
Lots of air the oceans and mountains
Bodega Bay sand cup hook
Waves can be heard and felt the whistle buoy also
Weimaraner puppy glad to see me again
Up beyond hope or wish or high
ZOP !

(Overtime 238)

Works Cited in A Dirty Bird in a Square Time

Allen, Donald, ed. Off the Wall: Interviews with Philip Whalen. Bolinas, CA: Four Seasons Foundation, 1978.

Butterick, George F. A Guide to the Maximus Poems of Charles Olson. Berkeley: University of California Press, 1978.

Dogen Zenji. Moon In A Dewdrop: Writings of Zen Master Dogen. Ed. Kazuaki Tanahashi. New York: North Point Press, 1985.

Olson, Charles. The Maximus Poems. Ed. George Butterick. Berkeley, CA: University of California Press, 1983.

Scalapino, Leslie. How Phenomenon Appear to Unfold. Elmwood, CT: Potes & Poets Press, 1990.

—. Introduction. In Philip Whalen, Overtime: Selected Poems. Ed. Michael Rothenberg. New York: Penguin, 1999. xv-xx.

Schelling, Andrew and Anne Waldman. "Philip Whalen: Zen Interview." In Disembodied Poetics, Annals of the Jack Kerouac School. Eds. Anne Waldman and Andrew Schelling. Albuquerque, NM: University of New Mexico Press, 1994. 224-237.

Whalen, Philip. Decompressions. Bolinas, CA: Grey Fox Press, 1978.

—. The Diamond Noodle. Berkeley, CA: Poltroon Press, 1980.

—. Heavy Breathing: Poems 1967-1980. San Francisco, CA: Four Seasons Foundation, 1983.

—. On Bear's Head. New York: Harcourt, Brace And World, Inc. and Coyote, 1969.

—. Overtime: Selected Poems. Ed. Michael Rothenberg. Intro. Leslie Scalapino. New York: Penguin, 1999.

Footnotes for A Dirty Bird in a Square Time

1 Whalen began meditating in the mid-50s and formal practice in Zen in 1972 (Allen 3, 71).

2 As comments on his early reading suggest, Whalen probably moved in this direction independently. He speaks of reading Lin Yutang's The Wisdom of China and India (1942) just after high school and Gertrude Stein's Narration during World War II (Allen 7, 16, 58, 69). That is, my point about Rexroth is debatable.

3 Whalen may be responding to Schopenhauer here, indeed Schopenhauer may be the source of Whalen's notion of a "world body," but the focus of these opening lines is on the nature of the World as an illusion, rather than World as an idea, as Schopenhauer argued.

4 The quote in parenthesis is likely from Schopenhauer—note the phrase "idea of emptiness"—but I could not locate the source.

5 In another poem written at this time, "I Am King Giant Dragon Sun," Whalen speculates "We are known by the character of those things to which we visibly / REACT?" Later he responds, "I don't belong to that and I don't belong to myself" (On Bear's Head 249).

6 The subject/object dichotomy he used, as mentioned above, is part of a Modernist legacy, and that paradigm also provides an important context for his remark that his poetry is "a picture or graph of the mind moving." You'll notice, for instance, there is a sense of scientific objectivity at play there, i.e. in the very idea of "graphing" the mind. (This is more evident in the full text, where he talks about the Wilson Cloud-chamber.) The statement is troubled by that notion of objectivity, for it seems to lack a sense of agency—Whalen wasn't simply recording thoughts; he was producing thoughts and then constructing poems from them, a selective process. But the importance of the statement is obvious.

7 Whalen himself makes this point in the preface to Decompressions (see for instance pp vii-viii).

8 See also The Diamond Noodle where Whalen talks of "conscious composition—interior direct report of internally heard speech (thought)...as now—as if another person were listening to me . . . ." (63).

9 At the conclusion of "Minor Moralia," Whalen writes of permitting all the repetitions, pauses, gropings to emerge, even those "which aren't actually necessary or real" (On Bear's Head 191). This kind of self-exploration, I'm arguing, was a deliberate project in the late 50s and early 60s.

10 Whalen made a related comment to Ann Waldman in a 1971, when he talked of discovering that a poem "could be what I was going to be or what it was going to be itself, and it started making itself and I started having to go along behind it and write it the way it was . . ." (Allen 1972, 22-3).

11 For anyone interested, I have an essay on Whalen's use of voice forthcoming in Sagetrieb.

12 The exasperation is also produced by word choice and phrasing, of course, for example, by the deliberately impatient way he asks "What's killing you now?"

13 Not to belabor the point, but in addition one might argue that scattered treasure from shipwreck of THE DIVINE MIND is likely to be illusory treasure. I should also mention, here, that there are odd parallels between "Tassajara" (1972) and poems by Dogen that Whalen helped translate several years later. See for instance Dogen, 218-9 (e.g. "When breakers are high, what kind of moon do you see?").

Acknowledgements

The editors of *Continuous Flame* have carefully researched the materials for this work, many of which were the property of Philip Whalen and are included in accordance with his wishes. In addition, we have made all possible efforts to obtain written permission from each known photographer whose work is included herein. We thank all who generously gave us permission to include their work. To any from whom we did not obtain permission because we had no identification or we could not locate a particular artist, your work was included because it was requested by Philip Whalen and we concluded that any friend or colleague of his would want to be included as part of this tribute to him. We hope to correct all omissions of attribution in the next printing.

Additionally, "Hiccups" by Robert Creeley originally appeared in *If I Were Writing This,* (New Directions, 2003); Duncan McNaaughton's "To Philip Whalen" is taken from the book, *Capricci* (Blue Millennium Press, 2003); Robert Winson's excerpt from *Dirty Laundry* appears by permission of Miriam Sagan; and "Flower Garland Froth" by Michael McClure was originally published by *Alsop Review* (© Jack Foley, July 2002), a fragment of "Flower Garland Froth" appeared in *Wind Bell,* 2002; "Fork Enso" by Nancy Victoria Davis previously appeared in *Mark Other Place,* a chapbook of Philip Whalen's poems (Big Bridge, 1997); "September 17: Airport Telephone Interzone" by Michael Rothenberg originally appeared in *Unhurried Visions* (La Alameda Press, 2003).

Special thanks to Anthony Bliss and the University Archives of The Bancroft Library, University of California, Berkeley, for their kind assistance. Much warm appreciation goes to Nancy Victoria Davis for her considerable work and care given to Philip's photographs reprinted within. As well, thank you to Allan Melville Chapin for legal council and for his enduring support of this project.